Cockroach

Animal
Series editor: Jonathan Burt

Cockroach

Marion Copeland

REAKTION BOOKS

Published by
REAKTION BOOKS LTD
79 Farringdon Road
London EC1M 3JU, UK
www.reaktionbooks.co.uk

First published 2003
Copyright © Marion Copeland

Printed in China

British Library Cataloguing in Publication Data

Copeland, Marion
    Cockroach. – (Animal)
    1. Cockroaches 2. Animals and civilization
    I. Title
    595.7'28

    ISBN 1 86189 192 X

Contents

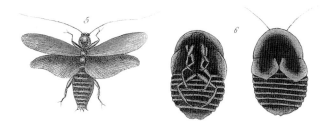

Two types of cockroach, from the first major work of American natural
history, published in 1747.

Introduction

The cockroach could not have scuttled along, almost unchanged, for over three hundred million years – some two hundred and ninety-nine million before man evolved – unless it was doing something right. It would be fascinating as well as instructive to have access to the cockroach's own record of its life on earth, to know how it survived when other species became extinct, to know its point of view on evolution and species dominance over the millennia. Such chronicles would provide, as Sue Hubbell has said, 'a very long view indeed'. Perhaps they would radically alter our perceptions of the dinosaur's span and importance – not to mention of our own development and significance.

The late Stephen Jay Gould points out in his Introduction to *The Book of Life* that the human narrative has virtually ignored the fact that invertebrates like the cockroach have continued to evolve ever since their appearance. Ninety per cent of all animal species on Earth today are arthropods. He warns that ignoring the history of such ancient, persistent life forms, pretending as we tend to that 'the twig of vertebrates', only 40,000 life forms strong, is the whole story, results in 'a seriously skewed account . . . Moreover, the bias thus introduced is the worst and most harmful of all our conventional mistakes about the history of our planet – the arrogant notion that evolution has a predictable direction leading toward human life.'[1] As one well-known cockroach remarked:

> i do not see why men
> should be so proud
> insects have the more
> ancient lineage
> according to the scientists
> insects were insects
> when man was only
> a burbling whatsit [2]

The cockroach chronicles will tell us that, throughout all these eons, the dominant visible life form has been and remains, if not the roach itself, certainly the insect.

Although the writings of naturalists and travellers record many cockroach encounters, attempts to chronicle the cockroach's intellectual and emotional life have been made only within the last century. In commenting on the effectiveness of the writings of John Crompton in bringing to life little-understood creatures like *The Hunting Wasp*, editor Stephen Bodio comments on the usefulness, even in so-called scientific accounts, of anthropomorphizing. Rather than seeing it as a sin, Bodio discusses anthropomorphizing as metaphor, 'a way of making the insects' way of life, as weird as that of Sigourney

Two cockroaches clearly reading their own history.

The comparative evolutionary history of the ancient and enduring cockroach and the relative new-comer, as shown in a Lippman cartoon

Weaver's "Aliens", comprehensible to the receptive human reader'. Thus he places the best naturalist writers, including Crompton, but one can add many others, beginning with Darwin himself, among those

> writers whose originality and sympathy have given us glimpses into the umwelt, the world view, of creatures other than our own kind, with the Kipling of the wonderful 'Mother Hive' story, with T. H. White's ants and geese and goshawks and badgers.[3]

Taking Bodio's lead, we will find most, although certainly not all, of the best insights into the cockroach in the evocations of artists who assume the cockroach is both sentient and intelligent and who therefore create cockroach characters, anthropomorphic or not, who tell their own story. Such works succeed by not just telling but showing the reader how cockroaches view the world, allowing them to participate in that world 'through the use of our imaginative faculties'.[4] The first modern examples, by artists as radically different as Franz

9

The *Animorphs* jacket shows Marco going through a morph from boy to cockroach.

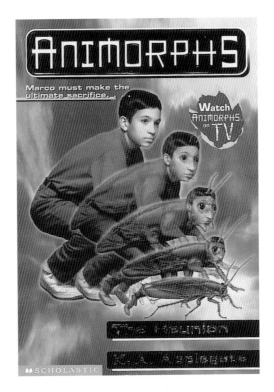

Kafka (1883–1924) and American writer and journalist Don Marquis (1878–1937), created equally memorable protagonists. Perhaps the most important thing about Kafka's Gregor Samsa (who is transformed into a nameless bug that most readers assume is a cockroach) and Marquis's *vers libre* poet archy is that each is allowed to tell his own story, giving us the cockroach point of view. The only fly in that ointment was that each had been human before metamorphosis in one case and reincarnation in the other transformed them into roach Gregor and cockroach poet archy.

A more radical step occurred when contemporary novelists like Marc Estrin, Donald Harington and Daniel Evan Weiss made unadulterated cockroaches the protagonists in their own life stories. Before that happened, Howard Ensign Evans, an entomologist, produced an essay, 'The Intellectual and Emotional World of the Cockroach', that suggests the sentience and complexity of the cockroach. The insect has no need to borrow either intelligence or emotional depth from humans, having by far the older wisdom and soul.

Since Evans, entomologists have developed the field of cultural entomology, the study of the involvement of insects in human food, literature, art, and music, which recognizes that the insect has been and is currently involved in just about every aspect of life in every human culture. More recently still, scholars in the humanities (and the sciences) became sufficiently biocentric to acknowledge that fictional cockroach chronicles like Marquis's *archy and mehitabel*, Estrin's *Insect Dreams*, Harrington's *The Cockroaches of Stay More* or Weiss's *The Roaches Have No King* might be as much about cockroaches as about humans.

Because humans and cockroaches seem in many ways not dissimilar life forms in such works, we find that, at least since Classical Greece, authors have brought cockroach characters into the foreground to speak not only for themselves but symbolically for all the weak and downtrodden, the outsiders, those forced to survive on the underside and on the margins of dominant human cultures. There is evidence that, because of that association, the cockroach may become one of the heroes of twenty-first-century ecofeminism, dedicated as that movement is to cleaning up the remains of the patriarchy along with reestablishing healthy, balanced ecosystems on Earth for all life forms.

Inevitably human myth and story apologizes for cockroach intelligence and literacy by humanizing cockroach characters as Kafka and Marquis do with Gregor and archy. But it is not inevitable that all human myth or story be unwaveringly anthropocentric. Not all human cultures have been anthropocentric. Not all modern human cultures are equally anthropocentric. In animistic thinking, humans or any animal can literally take on the forms of other living beings and, from that perspective, tell the other's story. Although cockroaches appear in stories worldwide, most as symbols – usually for something bad, a tendency magnified in the twentieth century by the use of the cockroach in exploitation films – some cockroach literature is, in essence, animistic. While most horror, fantasy and sci-fi movies have encouraged and exploited human fear and hatred of the cockroach, even a few of those films go beyond the expected, exchanging monster-making and fear-mongering for more positive cockroach portrayals.

For instance, the classic *Bug* (1975), based on Thomas Page's novel *The Hephaestus Plague*, has an entomologist hero. Before Professor Parmeter evolves into the mad scientist, he provides his students (and readers and viewers) with lessons in cockroach biology that promote appreciation of its survival instincts and long history and are essential to understanding the thematic thrust of novel and film. While *Bug* was without question intended more to scare than reform its audience's attitudes toward the cockroach, as Parmeter becomes obsessively involved with his roach experiments, the roaches themselves develop into, if not sympathetic characters, then victims worthy of sympathy whose instincts are to survive and return to their home in the bowels of Earth where they can exist without human interference.

The cockroach's story as well as its biology and history, seen from the perspective Parmeter suggests, can spark admiration,

BLATTARIA

however grudging, and, perhaps more important, 'affirm human kinship' with them. A biocentric reading of the human record as it relates to the cockroach, whether in the sciences or in the arts, translated to reflect the cockroach's own point of view, while revealing the natural history, myths and stories of this long-time resident of Earth, provides a lens through which I suggest we may come to share the cockroach's very long view. Although such a perspective is even more difficult to achieve in nonfiction than in fiction, I have done my best to present the cockroach from its own point of view. In this effort I join forces with a host of nonfiction writers like David Abram whose *The Spell of the Sensuous: Perception and Language in a More-than-Human World* tells readers how he first learned that 'insects – such diminutive entities – could have [great influence] upon the human species'; May Berenbaum whose *Bugs in the System: Insects and Their Impact on Human Affairs* reminds us that 'insects are ... the chief architects of terrestrial ecosystems' and that, wherever humans have ventured, we are 'latecomers, following in the six-legged footsteps of insects'; and Joanne Luack whose *The Voice of the Infinite in the Small: Revisioning the Insect-Human Connection* convinced me, as I hope to convince

A visual history of the cockroach from its fossil beginnings to the world it shared with the dinosaur to the urban world it shares with man, in a mural-like illustration by Brian Raszka (1999).

my readers, that cockroaches, biological and fictional, are in reality our elders, bringing us glimpses of a world we have all but forgotten, 'a dimension where our kinship with nature and other species has its roots'.[5]

In my final chapter, cockroaches are viewed from a perspective that can best be described as ecofeminist, a philosophy and political theory that combines ecological concerns with feminist ones, emphasizing 'the respectful, mutual relations that must be maintained . . . the reciprocity that must be practiced in relation to other animals, plants, and the land itself, in order to ensure one's own health and to preserve the well-being of the human community'.[6] Much in tune with those concerns, Steven Kellert concludes in 'Values and Perceptions of Invertebrates':

> we need to cultivate our sense of community with all living organisms . . . As [James] Hillman suggests [in *Going Bugs* (1991)], 'we must start not with their splendor – the horned stag, the yellow lion and the great bear, or even old faithful "spot" – but with those we fear the worst – the bugs.'[7]

1 A Living Fossil

The first volume of the cockroach chronicles is etched in the fossil rock of the Carboniferous Period, a period so rich in cockroaches – an estimated 800 different kinds – that palaeontologists have labelled it the Age of the Cockroach. The largest ($3^1/_2$ inch) complete cockroach unearthed so far was discovered by geologists from Ohio State University. It dates from about 300 million years ago, some 55 million years before the first dinosaurs. Unlike those preserved in amber in the Baltic and the Dominican Republic, it seems to belong to a species unlike any of the modern roaches. Living as well as fossil species are being discovered at the rate of about 40 per year.

Some of the best preserved early Cretaceous cockroach fossils, in a 'concentration of 385 insect specimens in a 20 inch (50 cm) square', have been found in southern England, by Ed Jarzembowski of the Booth Museum of Natural History, Brighton. The 'quality of preservation is outstanding down to the finest details of wing colors and veining and eye lenses'.[1] Such preservation is usually found only in amber specimens in settings as diverse as the Dominican Republic and the Baltic where subtropical rainforest trees, in response to stress or injury, produced resinous sap that, when fossilized, we know as amber.

Both Baltic and Dominican amber preserve cockroach 'inclusions' without flattening them and therefore specimens

In what is now the Czech Republic, some 320 million years ago giant insects hunted their prey in damp Carboniferous forests.

retain the distinctive ovoid shapes of ancient cockroaches and of the other creatures who shared the roaches' habitats 150–450 million years ago. As any dedicated Michael Crichton reader knows, amber has the additional advantage of preserving DNA as well as physical detail. While entrepreneurs will probably not rush to bring prehistoric cockroaches to life, we are learning a great deal about them and other ancient insects from their amber-preserved DNA. Thus amber plays as critical a role as rock in establishing the earliest chapters of the cockroach chronicles.

In *The Amber Forest*, George and Roberta Poinar have reconstructed both a vanished Dominican forest and the lives and activities of its denizens from evidence encased in thousands of pieces of amber mined there in the past few decades. Studies of fossil pollen, diatoms and other microscopic remains allow researchers to reconstruct long-ago landscapes and to determine how nature and, in time, human forces affected them. The work of palaeoecologists like the Poinars is to bring past environments back to life.

Each gem, they explain, contains a different individual with its own story to tell. Most of the 3,000 amber-entombed creatures examined are, like the 3 cockroaches and the many cockroach egg-cases (oothecae) among the Poinars' specimens, either bark-dwellers or winged. Both adult cockroaches and egg-cases are so well preserved that it can be clearly seen when they are hosts to parasite infestation. Many of the same

Two hairworm larvae caught in a desperate attempt to escape from the body of their cockroach host caught in a mass of resin.

parasites that bedevil modern wild cockroaches bedevilled these prehistoric specimens.

The Poiners found dramatic evidence of both benign hairworm and lethal wasp predation in fossil cockroaches. Recent theory suggests that parasites may choreograph the development of species. The prime example is the parasitic wasp. Several of the 200,000 species seem, since very early times, to have been tailor-made for predation on certain species of cockroach. It may be that the wasps and other parasites of the cockroach (or any organism) have tweaked the development of the host species to make them the perfect host.[2] The irony is that parasites, perhaps the cockroach's chief rival for the title of the world's most hated creature, have played a critical role in natural selection and the development of every species.

Another predatory drama told by Dominican amber, and still being enacted in neotropical forests in South and Central America as well as in African rainforests, casts the cockroach as victim of invading army ants (called driver ants in Africa). Although John Kricher downplays the danger of army ants in his *Neotropical Companion*, it is because he does not want to discourage travel. All other observers, including Charles Darwin (who also comments in *The Voyage of the Beagle* on cockroaches being stored as food for their larvae by hunting wasps), create army or driver ant scenarios worthy of the goriest horror movie. In Bahia Darwin observed 'many spiders, cockroaches, and other insects, and some lizards, rushing across a bare piece of ground' pursued by a swarm of small black ants who, surrounding them, caused 'the poor little creatures' to make 'wonderful' efforts to 'extricate themselves from such a death'.

Many travellers describe the swarming of these ants, noting that it brings disaster to practically all animal life that lies in their path. Few display the empathy Darwin expresses for the pain and terror of the ants' victims. The nineteenth-century naturalist Henry Walter Bates, for instance, assured his readers that

> The errand of the vast ant-armies is plunder . . . but from their moving always amongst dense thickets, their proceedings are not so easy to observe . . . Wherever they move, the whole animal world is set in commotion, and every creature tries to get out of their way. But it is especially the various tribes of wingless creatures that have cause for fear, such as heavy-bodied spiders, ants of other species, maggots, caterpillars, larvae of cockroaches, and so forth, all of which live under fallen leaves, or in decaying wood.

While Bates's observation that cockroaches are often found under the debris of the rainforest floor as well as in degrading wood is accurate enough, cockroaches do not have a larval stage, so what he assumed was cockroach larvae must have been some other species. However, some few species of cockroaches – and sometimes the females of winged species – are flightless and make easy prey for army ants. Their danger is increased by the fact that other insect eaters have learned to take advantage of the panic-stricken flight of the insects before the army or driver ants.

A little more than a hundred years after Bates wrote, Marty Crump sees her house in Monteverde treated to the army ants' cleaning service:

> Our house is literally alive with raiding parties . . . of reddish brown army ants with a mission – to grab every small

Cockroaches fleeing army ants.

living creature they can find. Thousands of ants march purposefully along the floor, up the walls, over the counters, and along the rafters. Before long they occupy every room in the house. Scorpions, crickets, and spiders frantically dart helter-skelter, but their escape tactics are futile.

Early evening we return to a clean house. Having secured the insects . . . as booty for later consumption, the ants have marched elsewhere . . . A great form of natural pest control.

Robert Sapolsky reports an equally useful invasion when his hut at the foot of Zenj, the highest peak in the Sudan, is over run with cockroaches. Because of the heat, he had extinguished the fire that kept the creatures confined to the thatch. It literally rained giant cockroaches, an invasion followed by an attack of army ants:

The place was swarming with them . . . They weren't bothering me . . . They were dismembering the zillions of roaches . . . and, horrifyingly, a three-dimensional bridge of ants, holding on to each other, had formed from the floor . . . pulling off the cockroaches, ten times their size.[3]

These modern encounters, like the Poiners' amber, help to bring to life the cockroach's fossil story.

It is hard, because the fossil evidence is so scattered, to determine where or when the cockroach originated. The cockroach may well have evolved before Carboniferous coal preserved it for our fossil record. Science writer Natalie Angier tells us in 'There is Nothing Like a Roach', that while fossils currently date only from 280 million years ago, 'some entomologists estimate that the creatures may have originated in the Silurian period, 400 million years ago'.[4] The only beings to challenge the cockroach as survivor-supreme are the '3.5 billion year old bacterium . . . called stromatolites' which survives in 'otherwise lifeless briny pools . . . in Australia' and 'millipedes – the first class of animals to dwell successfully on land 420 million years ago'.[5]

By at least the end of the Devonian era (360 million years ago), not far from the ocean shores, insects had evolved from arthropods such as centipedes and millipedes that had successfully made the transition from ocean to land. Insects and arthropods alike are descended from a single segmented ancestor, the wormish onychophoran which, like the cockroach, still shares the planet with us today. The cockroach's form evolved directly from the segmented form and simple anatomy of the onychophoran, a very functional and successful pattern. Bernd Heinrich suggests the value of coming to appreciate the insect's form since, being aware of the mystery of its form and function explains for him the sense of wonder he feels when he encounters so quintessential an insect as the cockroach.[6]

Current theory suggests that cockroaches emerged on either Pangaea, the original giant super-continent, or its daughter continent, Gondwanaland, which later split to become what is now South America and Africa, both still rich in cockroach species. The two continents split about 100 million years ago, creating the Atlantic Ocean between them and carrying two related cockroach stocks, each an estimated 30 million species, along with ferns and giant millipedes and dragonflies. The flooding that ensued when the continents split flattened the trees and formed the coal deposits, over 3,000 feet deep, that gives the Carboniferous period its name.

Evolutionary biologist Gary Galbraith describes Gondwanaland's Carboniferous environment: its 'air thick with dragonflies . . . on wings big as seagulls, and huge stoneflies,

A cockroach in 45 million-year-old Baltic amber from Blue Earth mines in Kaliningrad, Russia.

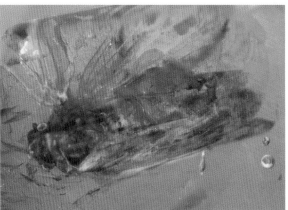

Ventral view of the cockroach found in Baltic amber. The cerci (appendages at the posterior of the abdomen) are oval in this wingless variety.

the ground stalked by springtails, cockroaches, scorpions, centipedes, millipedes'.[7] Plants had not yet learned to flower and the first grasses were still 20 million years from sprouting. Days were more like twilight and the sun glowed green through the leaves of plants like the thirty-foot-tall club mosses. Richard Fortey evokes the alien humid Carboniferous landscape in *Life: A Natural History of the First Four Billion Years of Life on Earth*, finding it already home to cockroaches:

> A splash catches our attention – a small crocodile, perhaps? Look more closely and you see other evidence of life. Two very large cockroaches scuttle rapidly away beneath the rotting stump of a tree-like fern. They flee the light, their antennae tucked away in darkness.[8]

Heinrich claims in *The Thermal Warriors* that the giant dragonfly *Meganeura monyi* had a wingspan of close to a metre and, with the cockroach, 'saw Triceratops and *Tyrannosaurus rex* come and go. These living fossils were so well adapted for flight soon after having evolved that we are forced to wonder whether improvements are still possible.'[9]

The size of these insects was made possible by the evolution of trees, which unlike the photosynthesis of the moss and algae that preceded them produced oxygen, causing Earth's atmosphere to become twice as rich in oxygen as it is today. With the later arrival of the mammals that recycled the oxygen, balancing the atmosphere with the carbon dioxide they produced, insects slowly grew smaller, until they reached the scale familiar to us today.

In 1869 T. H. Huxley announced that the cockroach was the archetypal insect, the model for all the species that developed after them. Beetles did not appear until 150 million years ago, butterflies, 60 million years ago. By the time they made their appearance, cockroaches were widespread and had already diversified to take advantage of Earth as it was then. Unlike either the trilobites or the dinosaurs, cockroaches – among those amazing creatures Darwin referred to as 'living fossils' – maintained a simple, practical form, evolved to profit from a variety of ecological niches and an equally simplified version of metamorphosis, which is misleadingly called incomplete because it lacks the larval and pupal stages familiar in moths and butterflies. Instead, the cockroach's growth process should be known as gradual metamorphosis. The narrator of Daniel Evan Weiss's novel *The Roaches Have No King* says, '*Blattellae* grow discretely. With each of our eight molts we jump from one size to the next. An instar is what we call a nymph, or youth, one who has undergone a particular molt.'[10]

Form and function as well as sheer luck have proven to be critical factors in the cockroaches having survived the great die-offs that marked the ends of the Permian period and Palaeozoic era (245 million years ago). Only an estimated five per cent of all species survived. Later, the cockroach also survived the extinctions of the late Triassic (208 million years ago) and Jurassic (144 million years ago), the 'K-T' dinosaur extinction, the late Eocene (37 million years ago) extinction, and the Pleistocene (*c.* 10,000 years ago) extinction of large mammals. Louis Barbier comments in 'The Cucaracha Wars', 'One has to think back and wonder what really drove the dinosaur into the tar pits. It might just have been the pesky cockroach.'[11]

In *The Roaches Have No King*, Weiss presents just such a fanciful but suggestive cockroach version of the extinction of their Jurassic neighbour the dinosaur. Cockroaches were particularly impressed by the power of *Tyrannosaurus rex*. In fact, Weiss's cockroach narrator, Numbers, tells us,

> Roach kids did not play Bats then, they played Tyrannosaurus. And not only did they emulate the beast, many of them lived off it. The spindly forelegs . . . could barely hold kills up to its mouth, so plenty dropped; more slipped between its huge teeth. Because of this, every Tyrannosaurus had an entourage of thousands of roaches.

This commensal relationship continued for thousands of years until one day in South Dakota, as 'thousands of *Blattela*, *Periplaneta*, and *Corporata* roaches were harvesting the falling blood and scraps' from a baby stegosaurus, one *Tyrannosaurus* took it into his head to 'stomp to death every one'.

The surviving cockroaches took this as a declaration of war and, with the *Corporata* leading the onslaught, proceeded to kill off first all of the tyrannosauri and then each of the other carnivores who claimed their place on the food chain by 'running into the dinosaur's nostrils and locking their bodies tightly together', effectively shutting off their oxygen.

'Ironically, the *Corporata* roach colonies soon collapsed under the weight of their organization and the species died out,' perhaps leaving its only trace in the closely related and successfully organized termite.[12] Whether present wild cockroach species will survive the current global extinction caused by deforestation which some experts believe 'rivals what occurred at the end of the Mesozoic era, 65 million years ago when the dinosaurs (and many other animals) became extinct', is another matter.[13] Many non-pest species of cockroach are seriously threatened today although, not surprisingly given human attitudes toward cockroaches, none have yet made the endangered species list.

Form was only one critical factor in the cockroach's success as a survivor. As Niles Eldridge points out in *Life Pulse: Episodes from the Story of the Fossil Record* (1987), other abilities were equally important. Among these were its reproductive prowess; its ability to withstand global cooling despite its tropical beginnings and its preference for warm, moist climates; its ability to deal with gravity; its rapid adjustments to changes in the magnetic polarity and oxygen levels of the Earth; its 'breakaway principal: we have fourteen points, two on each leg and one on each antennae, where we easily break; in danger's grasp, we can escape and leave the limb behind',[14] regenerating it at the next moult; and its ability to chew and digest almost anything from bark and leaves to paper and ink, from motor oil to leather and wool, from their own shed exoskeletons and empty egg-cases to insect and animal dander and skin, from bat guano to bread and Cheerios. L. C. Miall and Albert Denny add in *The Structure and Life Story of the Cockroach*: 'Cucumber, too, they will eat, though it disagrees with them horribly!'[15] More contemporary researchers 'have discovered that cockroaches' favorite food is glazed cinnamon rolls' and that they are also 'very fond of boiled potatoes and bananas dipped in beer'.[16]

The cockroach's essentially simple form consists of three bilaterally symmetrical body segments (head, thorax, abdomen). In fact, the Latin root of the word insect means 'to cut into', in other words, 'to segment'. In the roach, these segments are flattened and ovoid so they are able to slip into the smallest of cracks and fissures. Before the end of the Devonian period, the cockroach had discovered the advantages of six legs and of wings in enabling it to escape predators like the neighbouring giant millipedes and the giant dragonflies whose wingspan equalled that of the modern seagull, both of whom relished the taste of cockroach.

Wings were adaptations of the gills of aquatic mayflies and stoneflies. The roach's forewings are thick and leathery and serve as a cover for the diaphanous, net-like hind wings, which give their order *Dictyoptera* (Greek 'net-wing') its name. Unlike dragonflies, cockroaches evolved the ability to fold their wings flat against the body and are thus able to slip into tight places. Modern species have wing veins that differ from their fossil ancestors. A number of species since the Carboniferous have either lost wings altogether or, as in the German cockroach, adapted them for cosmetic and ritual uses during copulation and foreplay.

The cockroach's six legs are jointed and supplied with a multitude of tiny hair-like bristles (setae) sensitive to the slightest

Each leg has a multitude of tiny hair-like bristles, setae, sensitive to the slightest change in the environment. Equally sensitive ears are located in each knee joint.

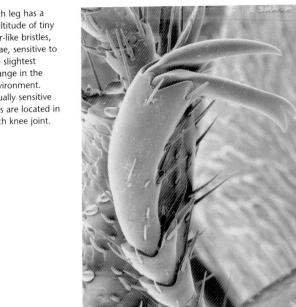

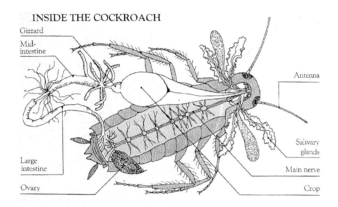

INSIDE THE COCKROACH

Gizzard
Mid-intestine
Antenna
Large intestine
Salivary glands
Ovary
Main nerve
Crop

Gerald Durrell's anatomy for aspiring naturalists comes complete with directions for catching, killing and dissecting the specimen.

environmental change, giving the roach both an early warning system and the speed and flexibility to exit a scene with amazing speed. The escape response of the cockroach has been clocked at 40 milliseconds (a millisecond is one-thousandth of a second). More extraordinary, the cockroach's ears, subgenual organs so sensitive they can 'distinguish earthquakes as small as 0.07 on the Richter scale', are located in each knee-joint.[17] Even more extraordinary are the adhesive or suction pads between the claws on the last leg segment, enabling many species of roach, like several of the more modern insect species, to crawl on vertical surfaces as smooth as glass. The pads automatically inflate when the claws are retracted, cling to even the smoothest surface, and deflate and detach as the insect moves.

The cockroach has grasshopper-like mouth parts for chewing 'far more adept than our own, with hard, chitinous jaws for chewing from side to side, maxillae with both soft and hard bristles for grooming his antennae and legs. Keeping antennae and limbs spotless [is] not just good breeding: his smell and vibrant senses would [be] compromised otherwise.'[18] The gut

Images made using electron microscopes can create both science and art, as here
by Tina Carvalho.

winds through the thorax (essentially the motor that supports the action of legs and the two pair of wings), meanders on through the abdomen, the largest of the three segments, and empties through the anus near the distinctive cerci. Cerci are the 'hairy feelers underneath the abdomen . . . that pick up vibrations in the air and warn of approaching enemies', an early warning system so powerful in the Madagascar hissing roach that the budding entomologist hero of Steven Cousins's young adult novel *Frankenbug* selects it as one of the attributes of his 'super bug'.

The cockroach's three body segments, encased in their exoskeleton (external spine) are further protected by a soft, slippery outer skin or cuticle which prevents it from becoming dehydrated and lubricates escapes into tight crevices. This lubrication is responsible for the distinctive odour that accompanies large congregations of certain species of cockroaches. Sperm and eggs are stored in the abdomen, which is segmented in order to be able to expand and contract. In fact, the cockroach abdomen is so supple and buff that fitness mavens have christened one abdominal stretching exercise the Cockroach!

The exoskeleton with its breathing holes or spiracles houses what scientists have come to realize is a complex chemical laboratory, producing chemicals used by the insect in defence, sex and communication. Though only a few insect neurohormones have been isolated for chemical analysis so far, it seems clear that they regulate virtually all body processes including growth, reproduction and metamorphosis. Chemical ecology, a relatively new field that studies the chemical relationships among living things, promises to reveal many of the secrets of insect scent language. For instance, chemical ecologists have discovered that when at rest many cockroaches secrete an aggregation pheromone, attracting other cockroaches to join them. The assumption is that as the number of resting roaches increases, the likelihood of someone sensing approaching danger mounts, thus benefiting the entire congregation.

Allen Moore of the University of Kentucky, working with a large, complex species of Tanzanian cockroaches, *Nauphoeta cinera*, has proved that pheromones determine the power structure in the stable social groups formed by this species. Not being a dominant male has definite evolutionary benefits in this forest-floor world since females, perhaps because they abuse them as well as other males, will not mate with dominant, aggressive males. Simply by stepping back and waiting, males whose pheromones induce passive, low status, inherit the females: 'Patience is a virtue', says Moore, 'even in the cockroach world.'[19]

With each succeeding molt or metamorphosis, the cockroach grows larger, bursts its exoskeleton and sheds it along with a number of internal structures, emerging as an almost white, vulnerable but very mobile nymph. Hardening of the exoskeleton returns the nymph to its particular species' colour and shape. These growth stages, called instars, are repeated until the nymphs reach adult size and therefore vary in number and complexity from species to species. Exoskeletons are often consumed by the cockroach and its cockroach neighbours for their protein value. The protein is efficiently recycled to produce new outer skeletons after moulting, hard coverings for the cases (spermatophore) in which the males present their sperm to the females, and the egg-cases (oothecae) the females form when ready to breed.

Both spermatophores and oothecae, many of which survive in the fossil record, are exceptionally well-designed and durable containers and explain, in part, the cockroach's success as a breeder, which comes not from the number of fertilized eggs produced but the care those eggs are given. Spermatophores are neatly wrapped in a protein-rich covering that provides the mother with the nutrients she needs to produce and brood her young. Cockroaches are the only insects to protect their eggs in oothecae, the distinctive and efficient hard-shelled, purse-like containers that the naturalist Gerald Durrell describes as 'elegant . . . little ladies' evening bags'.[20] Depending on the species, egg-cases contain from 14 to 28 eggs.

Some few species scatter their egg-cases around the neighbourhood, leaving their offspring, if the egg-cases survive predators and parasites, to fend for themselves. Most carry their oothecae with them, some few retaining it internally. Some withdraw it completely, while in others it protrudes but remains attached to the mother. Protruding cases are ejected when the young are ready to emerge. Retained and withdrawn cases allow for 'live birth' and usually in those species, parental care is prolonged. Several cockroach species are additionally capable of parthenogenesis and at least one species, *Pycnoselus surinamensis*, only propagates by what is essentially cloning. It is a species without males or sex, experiences live birth from eggs hatched within the body (ovoviviparous) and, not surprisingly, is decidedly maternal.

Other distinctive cockroach features are the pronotum or head shield – actually enlarged flanges of the thorax, from beneath which the head emerges, pointing downward in a distinctive and particularly cocky way – and the equally distinctive long, segmented, hair-like antennae. An antenna has 356 segments, each responsible for absorbing particular information from the cockroach's surroundings. Although we do not yet know what each segment monitors, the last 2 'have as their sole function an appraisal of [the cockroach's] own cleanliness, tidiness, and aroma'.[21]

The American cockroach (*Periplaneta americana*), with a

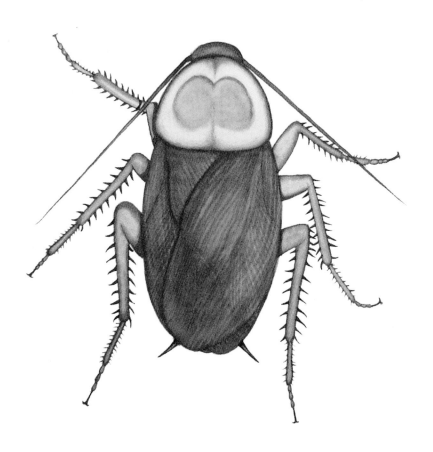

American cockroach (*Periplaneta americana*). Paintings of cockroaches by the naturalist Joe Bullock are a combination of scientific accuracy and highlighted natural detail.

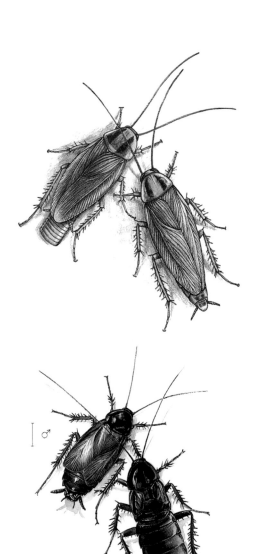

German cockroach (*Blattella germanica*). Amy Bartlett Wright accurately catches the identifying anatomical detail and colour variations of her pairs of subjects.

Oriental cockroach (*Blatta orientalis*). The gregarious Oriental roach, larger than the German Cockroach, is a shiny blackish brown.

body-length of three to four centimetres has antennae five centimetres long, enabling it to dodge obstacles at speeds faster than any other known creature. The head is distinguished further by two large eyes, which literally wrap around its front and sides. Not much escapes such vision, which, in addition to being multifaceted, takes in infrared and blue-green colours. As the narrator of Marc Estrin's novel *Insect Dreams: The Half-Life of Gregor Samsa* puts it:

> Vision for those with compound eyes is both less – and more – exact than for those with mammalian organs. While the overall image was somewhat blurry, a mosaic of soft focus like the surface of a Seurat, his [Gregor's] perception of motion was vastly more acute. As an image traverses from lens to lens, it ticks a sensor at each border that registers precise direction and speed. And so his peripheral vision was immense.[22]

German and Oriental cockroaches, like all nocturnal roaches, have 'sparkly . . . crystals on [their eyes] for hunting in the dark'.[23]

A parade of cockroach species in Janelle Cannon's children's book about her golden rainforest cockroach character, Crickwing.

Scientists are still puzzled by the speed with which stimuli detected by eyes and antennae reach the cockroach's legs. The resulting speed is the equivalent of a human running at the speed of 90 mph, a speed at which we would be unlikely to successfully dodge to avoid obstacles as the cockroach does. One researcher calls their nervous system 'beautiful'; another claims 'The most talented roboticist in the world is not going to come close to what a cockroach can do'.[24]

Living non-domestic cockroaches are beginning to be studied in depth by scientists who recognize their importance to the world's forests and ecosystems. Currently there are over 4,000 known species adapted to virtually every one of Earth's

Wood cockroach (*Parcoblatta fulvescens*). Amy Bartlett Wright's wood roach shares a range with the older, termite-like wood roach, *Cryptocercus punctulatus*.

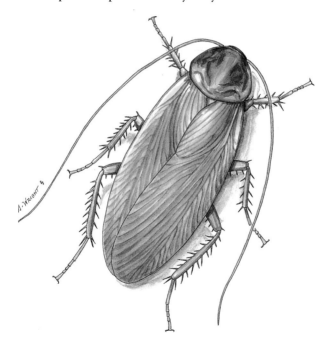

ecosystems. Quietly, unobtrusively, over the eons, the cockroach clan has spread to fill virtually every ecological niche, from tropical Edens to hardwood forests, grasslands, swamps and deserts, even polar regions. Today in La Selva, a typical neotropical rainforest, ten cockroach species studied recently were distributed from leaf litter to understorey. Three were consistently found only in the litter, four migrated from daytime perches in the understorey to feed in the leaflitter at night, and three perched and fed exclusively in the understorey.[25] Elsewhere there are species whose habitats are restricted to the interior of bromeliads or bamboo, to the splash zone of waterfalls, to ant and termite nests, to bat caves, to animal burrows (including ours!), and even to mines.

Cryptocercus punctulatus, a wild wood-roach living in the USA (there are 57 wild North American species, a dozen in Illinois alone), retains the image of its ancestors and chronicles for us what the life-story of fossil cockroaches may have been. As David Rains Wallace noted, it is one of 'a few species of . . . ancient insects native to the northern United States'. For him, its survival skills are a more valuable gift than glittering jewel-coloured wings, golden eyes or firefly 'lanterns'.[26]

Whereas many modern roaches have noticeably long antenna, *Cryptocercus* has short antennae, and its stocky, mahogany-hued body is typically flattened. It is about an inch (2.5 cm) long. Its sides are pitted with what are now assumed to be pheromone receptors. Nymphs in their first instars (the moults which facilitate the incomplete metamorphosis of the roach) closely resemble termites although the resemblance fades as each moult allows the insect to grow larger. 'Termites arose no later than the early Cretaceous period from cockroach-like ancestors not far removed from the living wood-eating cockroaches of the genus *Cryptocercus*.'[27]

Like termites, modern wood-roaches pass on to their young the unique cellulose-digesting protozoan symbionts that make it possible for them to survive on tough fibres of wood and bark. These microbes are themselves extraordinary beings. First revealed under the microscope in seventeenth-century Holland by Antonie van Leeuwenkoek (who called them 'animalcules'), they were first caught on film in the guts of wood-roaches from Mountain Lake, Virginia, by entomologist Lemuel Cleveland in the 1930s. He immediately guessed that they enabled the cockroach to digest a harsh, high-fibre diet.[28]

With each moult wood-roach nymphs shed their stomach lining and with it their wood-digesting symbionts, restoring the protozoan population by eating their parents' egg-laden droppings. Obviously, this keeps them at home and dependent on parental care until they are fully mature. Adult *Cryptocercus* mate for life, remaining in the tunnels they sculpt where they feed and provide for their single brood through the three to four years required for their offspring to reach their adult instar (moult), the imago. Their tunnels, like beehives, retain the constant temperature – in this case below 65 degrees Fahrenheit (18° C) – required to keep not the roaches but their internal symbionts alive. The young cockroaches begin to mate and shape their own network of tunnels at the end of their parents' five to six-year life span.

The hairy desert cockroach (*Eremoblatta subdiaphana*), another modern American wild roach, is indigenous to the Southwest. Like the brown-hooded wood-roach, this handsome reddish-orange species, only about an inch long, burrows and, again like its brown-hooded relative, is specialized to take advantage of its environment. Where the wood-roach has acquired wood-digesting symbionts, the desert roaches have refined the common ability of cockroaches to survive without

The easiest way to appreciate the size and shape of the Madagascar hissing cockroach is to see it in comparison to the size of a human.

water for two weeks or more by reabsorbing water from their own droppings into the ability to absorb water directly from the air, making it possible for these normally water-loving creatures to survive in the desert. The hairy desert cockroach also has slow-developing nymphs who remain dependent on the parents until fully mature, forming the kind of pre-social unit (family) that prepared the way for the social insects, the termites, ants and bees. As Gilbert Waldbauer explains, 'Group living at any level is important in the ecological scheme . . . because it enhances survival,' so, in fact, it becomes yet another of the reasons for the cockroach's success.[29]

In comparison to more recently evolved insects, the cockroach produces few young and lives long. The Madagascar hissing cockroach (*Gromphadorhina portentosa*) commonly lives for seven years, producing in that time fewer than twenty egg-cases which it retains internally, giving live birth, and defending its young. Thermoregulation, important in all insects, facilitates

essential activity such as flight and reproduction as well as aggression. The defence mechanisms of Madagascar hissing roaches – speed and a forceful hiss – are produced when fear causes blood pressure and the body temperature to rise. It comes into play as well when the hissing roach falls prey to *E. coli.* The infected individual exposes itself to sunlight – risking being spotted by birds or other predators – in order to raise body temperature sufficiently to kill the bacteria. Like all species of cockroach, they must conserve energy for such exertions by resting 75 per cent of the time, usually in sleeping aggregations, antennae at the alert.

Some of the more modern species of cockroach – usually only the males – are aggressive when their turf or possession of a receptive female is challenged, but most wild cockroaches prefer to slip away when danger threatens. Both male and

Catherine Chalmers's recent roach series are directly aimed at questioning human attitudes toward cock-roaches.

opposite: A
Kalenchae
cockroach,
from Catherine
Chalmers's
Imposter series.

female German cockroaches, one of the modern domestic roaches, will defend their egg cases (oothecae) and young from predators, which include many species of birds, lizards and mice as well as man. Some few species secrete defensive sprays capable of repelling predators such as ants, frogs and spiders. One of the tiniest wild cockroach species, *Attaphila fungicola*, has seen the protective value of symbiosis, serving as janitors in the nests of several species of leaf-cutter ants. Females ride on the backs of large soldier ants during their swarms, laying their eggs and raising their young in newly established nests after what David George Gordon in *The Compleat Cockroach* describes as their 'wild ride to other parts of the tropical forest'.[30]

Another wild species escapes being eaten by mimicking the red, black-spotted ladybird, which birds avoid, knowing it has poisonous blood. India's *Corydia petiveriana* avoids its predators by mimicking a fellow native chrysomelid beetle, while the Pacific Beetle Mimic Cockroach (*Diploptera punctata*), one of the cockroach species known to give birth to live young, imitates a small shiny brown beetle its predators have learned to avoid. Several species of beetle-mimicking roaches are found in New Guinea alone.

Still other cockroaches, noticed as early as 1874 by Thomas Belt, author of *The Naturalist in Nicaragua*, mimic the phosphorescent species of fireflies. Belt observed that instead of spending their time hiding in cracks and crevices and under logs as do most cockroaches, firefly mimics are freed to rest exposed during the day 'on the surfaces of leaves, in the same manner as the fireflies they mimicked'.[31] As Edwin Way Teale wrote in 1944, 'If you sat up nights trying to invent an indestructible bug, especially fitted to survive, you would have a hard time outdoing the roach.'[32]

2 What's in a Name?

Actually, there hasn't been an age since the Carboniferous that hasn't deserved the label 'Age of the Cockroaches'. Although 'We had no use for names in the sac,' comments Numbers, the cockroach narrator of Weiss's novel *The Roaches Have No King*, humans find it convenient to name the creatures inhabiting the world around them. Perhaps the need to name and classify had, at one time, a connection to shamanism and the magic of shape-shifting; in modern times it has become part of the human desire to dominate and control the natural world.

Since cockroaches exist in just about every part of the world, the domestic species have been observed and named in practically every modern and ancient human tongue: the Greeks and Romans, observing that cockroaches avoid the light, called them, respectively, *blatta* and *lucifaga*, meaning 'he who shuns the light'. In Chinese they are *chang-lang*. In Japanese, they are included among the *abula mushi* or night-singing insects and other beloved insects like fireflies, bees, cicadae and crickets. When associated with 'bad' insects like the millipede and hairy caterpillar, cockroaches become *gokiburi*.

Columbus called the cockroach *cucaracha*, from the Spanish *cuca*, caterpillar; the English versions of the name probably evolved from the Spanish since Francis Drake introduced the pest species to England in the 1580s when he brought a captured

Almost certainly, the earliest humans shared their shelters with cockroaches.

Spanish galleon over-run with roaches home to Queen Elizabeth. England has only three indigenous wild species – all wood-roaches. By 1624 the American colonist John Smith was referring to Drake's fellow traveller, who – nonpartisan – had accompanied explorers, Pilgrims and slaves to the 'New World', as *cacarootch*, and by 1657 Americans were calling the American domestic pest 'cockroche'.

Today 'cockroach' is the most widely spread common name, but pest species have acquired a veritable rogue's gallery of popular names. In Florida one native American cockroach is euphemistically called Palmetto Bug. Twice as big as the American cockroach, *Blaberus cranifer* cannot live further north and, measuring in at 3 inches (7.5 cm), gives Key West the

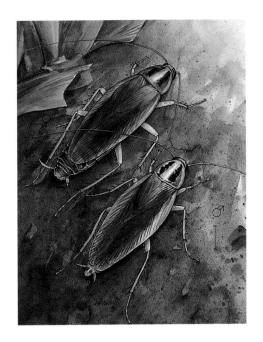

Asian cockroach (*Blattella asahinai*). Amy Bartlett Wright's depiction of this German cockroach look-alike, first identified on Okinawa in 1981, reveals that it indeed differs from the German cockroach.

distinction of being home to the biggest species of cockroach in the continental United States. Usually content to lie low and indulge its preference for leaves and grass, it seldom chooses to enter human dwellings. But even the visitor's guide admits that, after dark, the palmetto bug frequently flies, catching human attention by its size and colour.

Hawaiians, also impressed with the size and ability of the islands' cockroaches to fly and dive-bomb humans, refer to them as the B-52 cockroach, a name that inspired children's author Lisa Matsumoto to write *How the B-52 Cockroach Learned to Fly*. Her cockroach protagonist is determined not only to learn to fly but to prove that cockroaches, however humans demonize them, deserve a respected place in the insect kingdom.

LA CUCARACHA

Arr. A. G. W.

Allegretto

When a fel-low loves a maid-en And that maid-en does-n't love him,

It's the same as when a bald man Finds a comb up-on the high-way.

Chorus

The cu-ca-rach-a, the cu-ca-rach-a Does-n't want to trav-el

La Cucaracha ('The Cockroach') was, originally, a code name for the women who took part in the Mexican uprising of 1894. The song's lyrics are reprinted in the Appendix.

In 'I Began to Call Her Minnie' Gustav Eckstein notes that his groceryman, when he wants to de-demonize them, calls cockroaches May bugs. 'That is, if they are among the groceryman's apples they are May bugs', and goes on to note 'How much of human life that one-line fable sketches.'[1] The German cockroach is called a Crotan Bug in New York City because it first infested households there when water from the Crotan Reservoir was funnelled into the water supply in 1890. More often, popular names for the cockroach can be read as ethnic slurs, associating the pest with a particular unpopular group. *Blattella germanica*, known as the 'German cockroach' in the USA, is known as the 'Russian cockroach' or the 'French cockroach' in different parts of Germany and as the 'Prussian cockroach' in Russia, while the 'American cockroach' (*Periplaneta americana)* and the 'Australian cockroach'

(*Periplaneta australasiae*) both probably originated in Africa and not in the countries indicated by their common names.

> In Sweden [cockroaches] were known as *Brotaetare* or 'Bread Eaters'. In the UK the various pest species have been called 'Steambug', 'Steamfly' and 'Shiner' [as well as Black Beetle]. In America they are known as 'Yankee Settlers', 'Crotan Bugs' or 'Bombay Canaries' depending on where you are.[2]

Richard Schweid notes, among other negative uses of 'cockroach', that in the 1970s and 90s it was common for the Hutus in Rwanda to refer to the Tutsis as cockroaches, a reference reinforced by Peter Landesmon's article on the Rwanda minister of family and women's affairs, Pauline Nyiramasuhuko: Pauline is said to have called the Tutsi women she ordered Hutu troops to rape and kill 'cockroaches' and 'dirt' and to have referred to the genocide of Tutsis in terms of getting rid of cockroaches.[3] Similarly, in the 1980s members of the Israeli army and, more recently, Yitzhak Shamir called the Palestinians 'cockroaches'.[4]

So, clearly, it is not only the Americans surveyed by Stephen Kellert in this same era who found the cockroach the least appealing of all living things. As Schweid writes, 'if you want to say something nasty about someone, call him a cockroach: that lowest of the low, vilest of the vile, most easily eliminated without a pang of remorse, the cheapest of all lives, an animal only a Jain . . . would ever think twice about killing'.[5] No wonder novelist Donald Harington suggests in *The Cockroaches of Stay More* that even cockroaches prefer to be called 'roosterroaches', although he probably alludes more directly to the possibly mythical objection of certain prudish Americans to the 'cock' in the insect's common name.

The Yuckiest Site on the Internet, with its own cartoon mascot, Rodney Roach, is a delightful and informative site.

This linocut illustrates Robert Burns's verses 'To a Louse', another maligned insect species, in an illustration by Martha Paulos.

Like Little Miss Muffett, more disturbed by spiders than cockroaches, the British had by 1986 gone against the grain and founded a Blattodae Culture Group, complete with newsletter and web site, to 'promote the study and culture of cockroaches'. Americans, not to be outdone despite their rampant roach phobia, embraced Radar, one of the leading characters on the TV series *M*A*S*H**, who kept a zoo which included a cockroach collection of which he was particularly proud, and devoted a number of web sites, largely aimed at children, to the cockroach. *The Yuckiest Site on the Internet*, with its own cartoon mascot, Rodney Roach, is an excellent site even if it does tend to feature largely domestic 'pest' species.[6]

Better known is the symbolic role played by the cockroach in urban African-American life. 'Cock' is African-American slang for both penis and cop, and 'roach' for the butt of a marijuana cigarette. The latter association has been mainstreamed thanks to its link with the song 'La Cucaracha'. One of Theo's best friends on the popular TV comedy *The Cosby Show* was nicknamed 'Cockroach', and Jay Mechling notes that African-American kids in Philadelphia keep and race pet cockroaches.

More often, cockroaches in America are associated with disgust and fear. For instance, a recent video arcade game, 'Monsters on the Loose', presents as one of the adversaries to be overcome a hideous giant mutant flying cockroach. And to get to the Cockroach Picture Gallery hosted by the University of Nebraska at Lincoln, one must log-on at pested.unl.edu/roachind.htm. This explains why entomologist May R. Berenbaum, a champion of all insects, decided to host an annual Insect Fear Festival at Iowa State University. Hers is but one of many efforts to rehabilitate the image of the cockroach.

Naturalists and entomologists like Berenbaum have tended to be a bit less biased than the average Westerner in their naming of cockroaches. As one cockroach character in Daniel Evan Weiss's novel *The Roaches Have No King* says, 'in 1758 a chap named Carolus Linnaeus decided to tidy the living world. From the [Latin] word *Blatta*, which means 'shunning light,' he stamped out this classification: suborder *Blattaria*, superfamily *Blaberoidae*, family *Blattellidae*, subfamily *Blattellinae*, genus *Blattella*.[7] But Linnaeus was limited by the specimens available to him. For instance, the cockroach sent to represent the Americas was actually an invader from Africa, but he unwittingly called it the American cockroach as we do today. Its close African relative became the Australian cockroach in his scheme for the same reason, while the roach sent him from China, also an import from Africa, has ever since been the Oriental cockroach.

In England in 1665, ten years after Thomas Mouffet's *Theatre of Insects* was first published, Robert Hooke's *Micrographia* was

Mark Catesby's 1747 plate shows a Large-Crested Heron consuming a Spotted Eft; a chigger, two species of beetle, and (top) two species of cockroach.

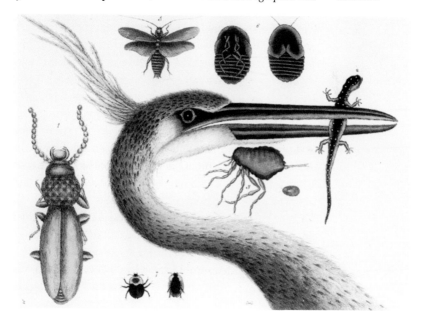

In England in 1658 Thomas Mouffet, the father of Little Miss Mouffett (and the author of the verses), accurately named the insect *Blatta*, describing the domestic cockroach in his *The Theatre of Insects*.

presented to the British Royal Society. Hooke's work is considered by many to be the best work of entomological illustration of all time. And his depictions and classifications have stood the test of time. When compared to modern scanning electron micrographs, Hooke's *Micrographia* is shown to be remarkably accurate in capturing the form and function of cockroaches and other insects. His cockroaches are creatures 'beautiful, intensely complicated and superbly adapted to their ways of life'.[8]

Until modern times, mammals and arthropods were classified by anatomy, habitat and reproductive strategies, but also by their value – or lack thereof – to man as food, medicine and symbol. Keith Thomas points out in *Man and the Natural World* that although many even in classical times viewed the natural world carefully and accurately, at the start of the early modern period in Europe and Britain most naturalists had what can only be called an anthropocentric view of the natural world. They classified all things, including the cockroach, according to its relationship to man.

One system, the 'doctrine of signatures', reflected the belief that everything worth categorizing had human use, and went so far as to assume that the creature's colour, shape and texture 'were designed to give . . . indications of that use'. Essentially, how they were viewed depended on whether animals were edible or inedible, wild or tame, useful or useless. Another, and, from a twenty-first-century vantage point, particularly insidious, categorization (not only for cockroaches) was aesthetic appeal or lack of it.

Apes, frogs, scavengers of all kinds, rats, reptiles, insects and amphibians were deemed ridiculous and loathsome looking. 'Reptiles, insects, and amphibians were especially detested, though the reason for this loathing was seldom clearly articulated. Modern anthropologists suggest that the explanation lies

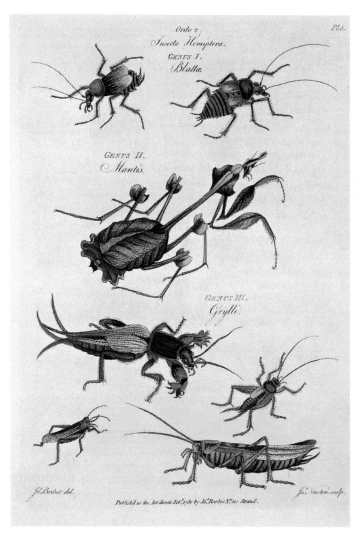

The mantis looks more like a leaf fairy, but the grasshopper and cockroach pair
is fairly realistic in this mid-19th-century illustration by James Newton.

In 1849, Charles D'Orbigny classified the Madeira cockroach (*Blatta maderae*) accurately and pictured it with other members of the order Orthoptera.

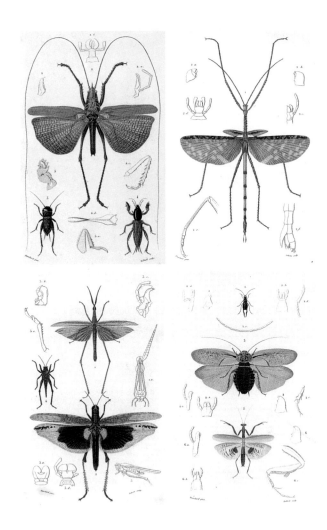

in their anomalous [not like us] status.' Zoologists at the end of the eighteenth century were still judging by this standard, so when zoologist William Bingby examined 'a human louse with the microscope, [he found that] its external deformity excites disgust'. The nineteenth-century Romantics, in some ways champions of the natural world, still saw nature as 'a mirror of human mood and emotions', failing to 'understand that . . . [it] was autonomous, only to be understood in non-human terms'.[9]

In *Waiting for Aphrodite: Journeys into the Time Before Bones*, Sue Hubbell explains that modern taxonomy – the science of classification and naming of the planet's life forms – had by the end of the twentieth century become more than a handy way of categorizing newly discovered individuals. The constantly refined classification schemes are a shorthand for 'everything heritable that is known about a particular animal and its relationship to all other animals'.[10] Revisions occur in order to make the system accurate as taxonomists discover new traits and relationships. The categories used are called taxa.

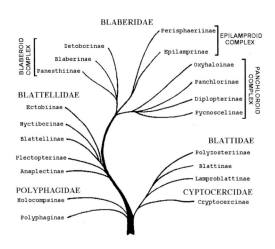

This cockroach Tree of Life (designed in 1954) appears on Joseph Kunkel's extensive Blattaria website.

Cockroaches, termites and mantids, all familiar members of the class Insecta, were first lumped with grasshoppers and crickets in the order Orthropoda, an error retained in a startlingly large number of contemporary field guides. Later the three were separated into the order Dictyoptera (Greek 'net-wing') because they are all characterized by net-like wings. The cockroach belongs to the suborder Blattaria, derived from the Greeks' observation that these were creatures that shun the light. Unlike roaches, Orthropods, and even the Dictyopteran mantids, prefer the sunlight.

There are currently 5 – though some insist on 6 – Blattaria families: *Blattidae* (with some 600 species), *Blaberidae* (with some 1000), *Blattellidae* (with over 1,750), *Polyphagidae* and the wood-roach *Cryptocercidae* (with 4 species). Fewer than 5 per cent of the known 3,500-4,000 living species of cockroaches that comprise these 5 families have been studied in depth. Most studies have been of those few domestic species man has known intimately, those who have become domestic pests. Both the *Reader's Digest Guide to North American Wildlife* and the Audubon Society's *First Field Guide to Insects* – as well as the Smithsonian's O. Orkin Insect Safari, an online and travelling natural history lesson for grade school children – include only the common domestic roaches, ignoring the continent's 57 known wild species. At least the Smithsonian has the excuse that its sponsor, Orkin, manufactures roach spray!

Whereas knowledge of beetles and butterflies has been pursued because humans admire the rich variety and colour of those insects, cockroach study has been motivated by human hatred. Much of that study has been devoted to finding better methods of extermination – something humans seem to take special pride in doing well. Even a cockroach behaviourist like Betty

Lane Faber, who has devoted hours to observing the roach in captivity and in the wild, admits her research is possible only because of pest control funding. It is sad that she has been unable to convince her supporters that studying cockroaches is its own reward. As entomologist Howard Ensign Evans puts it:

> to a student of roaches, it is self-evident that any creature so beautifully adapted and adaptable for [. . .] millions of years is worth lifetimes of study . . . if there are any underlying principles of long-term survival, surely they are evidenced by the roaches.[11]

Faber herself says that studying 'the wild roaches of Trinidad, whose jungles spawn about 200 species', is 'sort of like science fiction. If I were going to Mars, and I was looking at some creature I didn't understand, where would I start? That's how I try to treat cockroaches.'[12] PBS's recent *Alien Empire* makes much the same observation. Rushing to explore outer space, we ignore the 'aliens' in our midst, demonizing them whereas we often romanticize as well as demonize extra-terrestrial life.

Since it is very clear that funding for cockroach research flows from human desire to control and exterminate them, neurohormone research will probably be well funded. A recent discovery that the leaves of an endangered mint plant produces an effective roach repellent will undoubtedly ensure the protection of that plant's habitat. At least contemporary methods of control attempt to avoid the massive and indiscriminate use of insecticides that became the hallmark of effective cockroach extermination in the 1950s and remained its hallmark well into the 1990s.

The winner of Australia's 1991 Inventor of the Year award came up with an electrified version of the roach motel. After the

The beleaguered urban cockroach, whose sympathizers include both poet Barry Louis Polisar and illustrator David Clark.

cockroaches are lured in to stuff themselves with the bait, they 'end up fried'. More organic is a roach motel the EPA is considering that uses parasitic worms, harmless to humans but deadly to roaches, with the compassionate assurance that once all the cockroaches 'are eaten, the worms die because roaches are the only thing they'll eat'.[13] Heinrich suggests that since the pest species, all of tropical origin, are not able to survive in cold climates, relying on the heat we provide to sustain them in cold climates and seasons, and since the arsenal of chemicals we have launched against them have been only temporarily useful (and deadly to many others including ourselves), we simply turn off or, depending on the climate, turn up the heat, freezing or frying our unwanted guests.

The method worked in Yale University's Beinecke Rare Book and Manuscript Library, where the optimal temperature

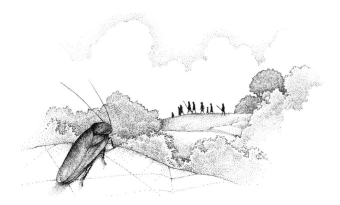

The moment that belongs in the foreground of human evolutionary history . . . as imagined by Janelle Cannon.

and humidity not only preserved old papers and leather but fostered the well-being of book-eating beetles, book lice, silverfish, termites and cockroaches. Imposing a temporary deep-freeze did little to harm the Library's collection and killed the 'pests' and their eggs. The powerful US pest control industry took immediate action against the use of heat or cold as a method of extermination, but Heinrich hopes to see thermal control as the wave of the future: 'We'll be thermal warriors [like the insects], using the very methods to control insects that some of them use on *their* enemies. Then we'll not only have learned about insects, we'll have learned from them . . . After all, they already know what works – they patented it millions of years ago.'[14]

Knowing their natural history should lead us, as David George Gordon puts it in the preface to *The Compleat Cockroach*, to 'regard the cockroach in a new light. Instead of an accursed nuisance, we are seeing a wizened old soul – one whose ancestors were around when the continents were formed, who witnessed the emergence and disappearance of the dinosaurs, and who watched an agile, chimpanzee-like primate become *Homo sapiens*.'[15]

3 Fellow Traveller

When written rather than fossil records become available, those keeping them are already modern humans and the vast majority of references to cockroaches come from Western humans, familiar only with the so-called pest species and already deeply biased against the creatures. What the journals and letters and published works of explorers and travellers provide are essentially personal encounter narratives written as they busied themselves 'discovering' and claiming and exploiting the world – invariably accompanied by what are now the most widely spread species of 'pest' cockroaches.

Although cockroaches do not migrate, they participated, long before humans provided them with luxury accommodation, in what entomologists call 'evolutionary dispersal', carried along by shifting tectonic plates as continents split and joined, as well as drifting on debris from one shore to another. Much later they also quite literally hitched rides with human travellers and explorers, attracted to their supplies, and eagerly adapted to new territory. Eventually cockroaches came to be anticipated, if not graciously received, fellow travellers. Webster's Third *Dictionary* defines 'fellow traveler' as one who sympathizes with, even furthers the ideals and aims of an organized group without being a member of that group.

Slave ships as well as space ships are said to have carried

Cockroaches are 'painted with the image that festooned Columbus's sails', In *Hello, Columbus* by photographer Catherine Chalmers.

more than their share of cockroaches along with their human cargo, leading to an early association of cockroaches and slaves. It is established that the American cockroach arrived via the slave routes, probably from Africa. *Periplaneta americana* has since then become 'part of the local invertebrate fauna' throughout the human inhabited world. In fact, in the 1920s 'a sizable population . . . turned up . . . thriving at a depth of 2,166 feet' in a mine in South Wales, finding the *déjà vu* Carboniferous atmosphere quite as pleasant as the bowels of London or New York.[1]

Travel literature is replete with cockroach encounter tales. From it we learn that sailors staged the first cockroach races to while away hours of shipboard boredom much as the war-weary doctors on *M*A*S*H* did. Cockroach races continue to provide distraction today. They are so popular in Brisbane, Australia, where The World Champion Cockroach Races have been held every January since 1982, that they are included in tourist brochures, featured on local web sites, and listed as a must-not-miss in Dave Freeman's *100 Things to Do Before You Die*. A typical year draws a crowd of 6,000. Australians, who wonder themselves about their affection for the cockroach, recently nicknamed popular cricket player Greg Atherton the Cockroach. The Queensland giant cockroach (*Macropanesthia rhinoceros*) – all 30 gm (1.06 oz) and 8 cm (3 inches) of it – is a popular pet, selling for $50 a pair and featured fondly on a government web site.[2]

The prize for spectacle has to go to 'bugrace99' at SYMPOSIUM ARS ELECTRONICA 1979–99, in Linz, Australia where, not the cockroach racers but the race course itself was bugged with mechanical electrical stimulations. Enthusiastic betting accompanied each day's heat and, on the final day of the extravaganza, the bugs that had won each day competed and the fastest cockroach was crowned.

In the United States, where roaches are admittedly less loved, races at Roachill Downs none the less enliven Purdue University Entomology Department's annual Spring Fest. Although the official claim is that it is a vehicle used to inform avid fans about the role of the roach in nature and to clarify notions about roaches as pests, the 'All-American Trot' has become a crowd-pleasing spectacle. In addition to the races themselves there is a tractor-pull in which teams of large Madagascar hissing roaches pull miniature tractors while spectator cockroaches – all dead, posed and dressed – cheer them on, a touch inspired no doubt by the example of Richard Boscarino, the creator of 'cockroach art' and of the dioramas at

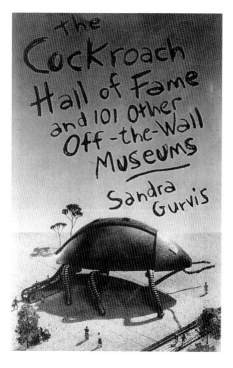

The Cockroach Hall of Fame, located just north of Dallas, Texas, features only the American cock-roach (*Periplaneta americana*).

the Cockroach Hall of Fame in Plano, Texas. One hopes the Hall never hears about the fighting cockroach parlours of Rangoon that Mark Leynor describes in *Tooth Imprints on a Corn Dog* (1995).

By far the most significant, if not the most spectacular, of cockroach races in the United States is the one held prior to each presidential race by the New Jersey Pest Control Association. Every four years its annual Cockroach Derby becomes a predictor of which Democratic presidential candidate will emerge the victor. In 1999 Al Gore outran Bill Bradley and in 1992 Bill Clinton 'won by an antenna'.[3]

An allusion to cockroach racing – and an interesting one – is found in the 1995 film *Race the Sun* in which there is an international solar-powered race-car competition. The Hawaiian entry is named 'Cockroach', and its design, inspired by seeing a cockroach run across the room, is described early in the film. The boy designer explains that he designed the car to look not unlike a cockroach, hoping to capture the organic, aerodynamic shape that first inspired cockroach racing and later made the insect the model for movement studies that spawned robo-roaches.

More recently, traditional cockroach racing has come to American TV thanks to the popular series *CSI: Crime Scene Investigation*. In a May 2002 episode called 'Ellie', the chief investigator, forensic entomologist Gill Grissom, is off to an entomology conference, leaving the staff to solve the weekly murder and taking with him his substantial glass container of carefully bred, carefully trained Madagascar hissing racing cockroaches. Apparently the major event at the annual conference is a highly competitive cockroach race and this year, Grissom tells his bemused colleagues, he is determined to win the gold. Not until the case is solved does he reappear, crestfallen, to announce that his racers had come in second, third and fifth.

It's easy to see why most sea voyagers did not welcome the cockroach as fellow traveller. Captain Bligh's HMS *Bounty* was, at one point, so infested with roaches – apparently non-racing roaches – that he ordered the ship totally disinfected with boiling water. Numerous other travellers' reports confirm that such shipboard infestations were common – no wonder, really, if these ships used for ballast, as did *The Lady Julian*, a three-masted schooner carrying female convicts from London to New South Wales in 1790, a mixture of sand, gravel and human waste that must have struck roach travellers as a treat only to be equalled by a cave of bat guano or an archipelago of bird droppings.

The Roach Crossing Sign actually deserves display around the world.

Mark Twain set off as correspondent for *The Sacramento Union* to the Sandwich Islands, now the state of Hawaii, in March 1866. Bound from one island to another on the schooner *Boomerang*, Twain first complains about an annoying rooster that crowed most of the night, then about a rat, and then about a series of fellow travellers who galloped over him in his coffin-like bunk:

> I thought it might be a centipede because the captain had killed one on deck in the afternoon. I turned out. The first glance at the pillow showed me a repulsive sentinel perched upon each end of it – cockroaches as large as peach leaves – fellows with long, quivering antennae and fiery, malignant eyes. They were grating their teeth like tobacco worms, and appeared to be dissatisfied about something. I had often heard that these reptiles were in the habit of eating off sleeping sailors' toenails down to the quick, and I would not get in the bunk anymore. I lay down on the floor. But a rat came and bothered me, and shortly thereafter a procession of cockroaches arrived and camped in my hair. In a few moments the rooster was crowing with uncommon spirit and a party of fleas were throwing double somersaults about my person in the wildest disorder, and taking a bite every time they struck. I was beginning to feel really annoyed. I got up and put my clothes on and went on deck.[4]

Twain's experience led to his writing 'Results of Kindness to a Cockroach', printed in *Practical Jokes with Artemus Ward, Including the Story of the Man Who Fought Cats* (1872), which reflects the same attitude toward cockroaches as reflected in his letters to *The Sacramento Union* quoted above.

In a fictional account based on Twain's experience, contemporary novelist Dan Simmons imagines a journey shared by Twain and the famous nineteenth-century traveller Isabella Bird. His fictional Twain mentions that his cabin mates were 'as big as peach leaves' and that they had 'fiery, malignant eyes'. Bird, as the two share encounter stories, responds that her visitors were 'lobster sized' and 'appeared to be plumping my pillow in preparation for a long nap of their own'. She had decided to leave them her cabin when the smaller of the two seized the parasol she sought to use to defend herself from them. Twain replies that it is best not to do battle with what have grown in the course of the conversation into 'reptile-sized insects'.[5] While the encounter and some of the exchange takes some artistic licence, Simmons obviously had read both Bird's and Twain's accounts and used them to create the flavour of the nineteenth-century Pacific journey for both cockroach and human traveller.

An indomitable traveller, Isabella Bird confirms Twain's shipboard cockroach encounters in *Six Months Among the Palm Groves, Coral Reefs and Volcanoes of the Sandwich Islands* (1890). Earlier, in *The Golden Chersonese* (1879), Bird narrates her travels from Japan to China and from China to the Malay Peninsula. Aboard the SS *Rainbow* from Singapore to Malacca, she finds her cabin uninhabitable: it was a small, very hot, dirty hole, 'tenanted by cockroaches disproportionably large'. On the *Rainbow* again later, she would find the cabin hotter still and swarming 'not only with mosquitoes but with cockroaches, which in the dim light looked as large as mice'.[6] As Simmons suggests, she chose to sleep on the bridge and avoid these fellow travellers who, at least in this narrative, seem to have no presence on shore, although mosquitoes, centipedes and ants of many species occasion much comment, most of it negative. She is, on the other hand, quite charmed by singing crickets and colourful butterflies and moths.

Early in the twentieth century, Jack London, like Melville and Twain, sailed the South Pacific on the *Snark*, finding as they did, that he had cockroaches as companions. He first comments on those encountered off Suava on the *Minolta*:

> The cockroaches on board held a combined Fourth of July and Coronation Parade. They selected midnight for the time, and our tiny cabin for the place. They were from two to three inches long; there were hundreds of them, and they walked all over us. When we attempted to pursue them, they left solid footing, rose up in the air, and fluttered about like humming-birds. They were much larger than ours on the Snark. But ours are young yet, and haven't had a chance to grow.

Later in the voyage on his own schooner, its crew plagued by tropical ills, London – one of the few tropical travellers to appreciate the survival skills of the cockroach – noted: 'Only the cockroaches flourish. Neither illness nor accident ever befalls them, and they grow larger and more carnivorous day by day, gnawing our finger-nails and toe-nails while we sleep.'[7]

In a similar vein, writing from her prison cell in Tahiti in 1990, the protagonist of Ronald Wright's *Henderson's Spear* observes

> The washbasin in my cell is a mixed blessing – no plug or trap to keep down the smells and cockroaches. Until Pua showed me the remedy (chewing gum and a coin), I thought I might be gassed in my sleep or nibbled raw. Tahitian roaches are as big as mice and they go for the dead skin on your feet.

I don't mean to make too much of these discomforts. My hotel in Papeete was much the same, at ninety dollars a night. In French Polynesia they know how to let off nuclear weapons but they've never grasped the rudiments of plumbing.

By the end of her internment on a false charge of conspiracy, the cockroaches have grown 'big enough to ride on'.[8]

Eighteenth- and nineteenth-century naturalists like Mark Catesby, Henry Walter Bates and Alfred Wallace also report on cockroach encounters. In 1747 Catesby, in *The Natural History of Carolina, Florida, and the Bahamas*, called the cockroach 'very troublesome and destructive vermin . . . so numerous and voracious that it is impossible to keep victuals of any kind from being devoured without close covering. They are flat and so thin that few chests or boxes can exclude them . . . It is at night that they commit their depredations, and bite people in their beds, especially children's fingers that are greasy.'[9] The reports do not get much more complimentary.

Bates and Wallace explored the Amazon Basin, a wilderness as strange to them as outer space. Stopping on the Para River at the home of Senhor Seixas, the two were housed in a room that had formerly been used to store cacao and were kept awake 'for hours by rats and cockroaches, which swarm in such places. The latter', Bates wrote in *The Naturalist on the River Amazon*, 'were running about all over the walls; now and then one would come suddenly with a whirr full in my face, and get under my shirt if I attempted to jerk it off.' Bates also found the settlement of Altar do Chao on the Tapajos River swarming 'with vermin; bats in the thatch; fire ants . . . under the floors; cockroaches and spiders on the walls.'[10] In most of their 'bed and breakfasts', the two explorers encountered pet geckoes, lizards that, like the cockroaches, are most active at night and greedily consume cockroaches.

In São Gabriel da Cachoeira, Brazil, on the upper Negro River, mid-nineteenth-century botanist-explorer Richard Spence found the old house he rented 'stocked with rats, vampires, scorpions, cockroaches, and other pests to society', while the earth floor was 'undermined by *sauba* [leafcutter] ants . . . In one night they carried off as much farinha [the manioc flour that is an Amazonian staple] as I could eat in a month; then they found out my dried plants and began to cut them up and carry them off.'[11]

A century and a half later, when naturalist writer Sy Montgomery journeyed on the Amazon and its tributaries in quest of the fabled pink dolphin, she found cockroaches still so much a part of camp and village life that her group's morning routine began with 'shaking our shoes out, evicting giant cockroaches'. Like Bates, she experienced some who 'jumped in my face and then ran down my arm'. While not enjoying their company Montgomery and her crew take their presence in good humour, flicking them away 'like some kind of insect badminton'.[12] Montgomery's contemporary Marty Crump, searching not for pink dolphins but for golden frogs, first mentions neo-tropical cockroaches as a component of the lyrics composed by her research assistant to celebrate her twenty-fifth birthday in 1971: home on the range 'where cockroaches roam' certainly describes their kitchen in Munozlendia where the insects scuttle 'across the dishes, the counter, the table, the [birthday] cake', leading Crump to comment that 'they act superior, as if they know they'll rule the earth someday'.[13]

The response of British naturalist author John Crompton (J.B.C. Lamburu), usually the champion of the creatures most people hate, to the cockroach epitomizes the average traveller's feelings. First encountering the cockroach when he served in the Rhodesian Mounted Police and later in India and China, he wrote in *The Hunting Wasp*:

The flat, obscene cockroach, with its nauseating smell, that squeezes horribly into narrow crevices is – to me – something straight from a nightmare. On hot seas some steamers are riddled with them. They come out at night in unspeakable slithering masses and eat the refuse and get in bunks and nibble toenails and hair. Cockroaches and rats: can you have a fouler combination? I am prejudiced against them, I know – if one can be prejudiced against what is entirely vile. I am prejudiced because I have traveled in dirty steamers in the tropics in China and because I have slept in filthy Chinese inns where – with the rats – cockroaches made night a purgatory.

Crompton's loathing, however, surely rose in response to the encounter he had in Rhodesia when on a murder investigation. Arriving at the native kraal where the body had been placed in a windowless hut, awaiting the medical examiner, Crompton and his companions entered to find the corpse shimmering and moving as the horde of cockroaches that covered the corpse fled,

covering first the floor and then the walls, squirming wildly into cracks and crevices and hanging in obscene knotted struggling ropes. Soon they were gone, save for the odd ones hiding here and there and dashing for safety every few minutes. We had got accustomed to the dimmer light and could see. The corpse had not the external appearance of the corpse I had . . . inspected. The entire skin . . . was pitted and gnawed and corrugated like wave-marked sand and this included the scalp from which all the hair had been eaten.[14]

Cooler heads, of course, could see this as an example of why forensic entomologists today use insect evidence to determine time of death and, often, to give clues to the cause of death, but Crompton's response, not surprisingly, simply expresses what has become the Euro-American 'repulsion' and 'dread' of the least-loved of all creatures.

At home and abroad, cockroach encounters continue to embellish travel literature. Pamela Petro, in *Sitting Up With the*

Cockroach phobia makes the insect a frequent visitor to the set of reality-based pro-grammes like NBC's *Fear Factor.*

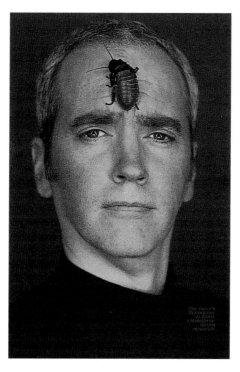

Dead: A Storied Journey Through the American South (2002) encounters motel cockroaches so huge she prefers to sleep in her car. A twenty-first-century Peace Corps volunteer in Kenya uses cockroach encounters as the focus of her experiences there. Calling her online journal 'The Cockroach Caper', Jeanne Daigle begins her tale at her 'homestay' in Naivasha, Kenya, where the kitchen is over-run with cockroaches, but the pace really picks up when she reaches her assigned site where cockroaches share her bed and live happily in the vinyl cushion of her chair. In Kenya, she concludes – and is seconded by Kenyan novelist Meja Mwangi (*The Cockroach Dance* 1979) – one lives cheek by jowl with one's cockroach neighbours.[15]

Travellers to what Peter Tyson calls the 'Lost World of Madagascar', an island large enough to be, as he suggests, the eighth continent, encounter a world left isolated off the southeast coast of Africa since the middle Cretaceous about 100 million years ago – 'a chunk of Gondwana preserved down to the present day'. 'Madagascar is a place', Tyson writes, 'where lizards scream, giant cockroaches hiss, and a handsome beast called the indri sings a song of inexpressible beauty.' In the Spiny Desert, 'looking for a species of nocturnal gecko that spends the day sleeping on tree trunks', Tyson peeled 'back a strip of bark only to scare up a seething mass of tarantulas, scorpions, and giant hissing cockroaches'.[16] The species, now familiar to Westerners from zoos and nature programmes and pet stores, is indigenous nowhere else.

Not all travellers were as disturbed by their roach encounters as Crompton, Twain and Bird seem to have been. In *The Amateur Naturalist*, Gerald Durrell recalls his childhood on Corfu. Although his mother 'waged a constant unsuccessful battle' with the two local species of cockroach that shared the warmth of the family villa's big stone kitchen, ten-year-old

Gerald was 'fascinated by their beauty'. To him 'they looked as though they were carved out of tortoise shell' and he collected their 'elegant' eggcases, hatching them (without his mother's knowledge) in his room. Feeding half of them to his other pets, he consistently let the other half go in the house and grounds, feeling 'this was fair'.[17] But then Gerald was both a child and a nascent naturalist, not a normal human being like Twain.

Elisavietta Ritchie writes of an experience in Malaysia, that took place the year her twenty-three year marriage was dissolving, in which she finds comfort in the presence of a cockroach. Alone, late at night in a hotel, writing, she realized she was being observed by a large cockroach. Every night the creature hovered nearby, keeping her company when no one else would. From it she learned the value of retreat when one is threatened, of surviving in a crack, of patience, of avoiding the glare of the sun, and of resuming your station when conditions become less threatening. And she was grateful for its presence.[18]

When Brenda Marshall and her husband spent a few weeks in Brazil they had a cockroach encounter that almost began fatally for the cockroach who was in the drain of the tub which they filled with very hot water. Rescuing him (or her), they thereafter chose tepid baths and soon thereafter a cockroach walked from the bathroom to the husband's chair. Marshall fed the creature tiny pieces of hard-boiled egg. Apparently it liked either the egg or the company or both, for it returned on several evenings during their stay.[19]

Similar stories emerge from the concrete jungles of New York City and Washington, DC. When Richard Schweid was twenty-one, he bunked in Greenwich Village with a host of hippie friends, all 'determined to save not only our own asses but those of our friends, neighbors, and every sentient being'. The nearest nonhuman sentient beings were the cockroaches in their apartment, who were numerous enough to require periodic visits from the exterminator. After one such purge, Schweid woke to find his

> body . . . a charnel house, a killing field of dead and dying roaches that came out from . . . their sanctuaries . . . in confusion as their poisoned bodies broke down . . . They died slowly, on their backs, legs kicking feebly in the air.[20]

The horror of their suffering rather than a horror of cockroaches is what haunted Schweid and led years later to his writing *The Cockroach Papers: A Compendium of Literature and Lore.*

In Washington, 'a famous gathering place for cockroaches', '[t]he best roaches', according to poet Elizabeth Fallin-Jones, 'have houses in Georgetown.' Journalist Bob Arnebeck, doing the dishes in the Capitol district late one night, noticed a very large cockroach crawl from behind the sink to watch him do the dishes. He soon found himself talking to it, fancying that its 'long, elegant antennae' were swaying in 'a communicative way'. The roach returned often, sometimes bringing friends, no more than three, along. Although the creature seemed not to like Arnebeck's wife joining them, after she gave birth it often appeared in their bedroom when the three Arnebecks were snuggled up in bed. 'We couldn't help but admire its curiosity,' he wrote, adding that he saw 'the moral of the story' as being 'that cockroaches are homebodies, water drinkers, eat what you eat, and care about your wife and kids. And with those very long antennae also have a gift for listening.'[21]

Arnebeck, who had contributed to the *Washington Post*, submitted the story, but the *Post* seemed uninterested in carrying a story about coming to appreciate the finer qualities of the cockroach. It is worth noting that such appreciative receptions are almost always the result of encounters with individual cockroaches – Eckstein's Minnie is another case in point – rather than mass encounters, which may explain why literary works that have named cockroach protagonists and/or narrators become such effective vehicles of attitude change while horror films tend to inflict hordes of cockroaches on audiences.

A traveller who likes cockroaches alone and *en masse*, John Kricher, author of the popular and useful *A Neotropical Companion*, describes several encounters with the 'Cockroach with the Divine Face', *Blaberus giganteus*. Approaching one of these 10–15 cm (4–6 inch) beauties with its 30 cm (12 inch) wingspan in Amazonian Peru, he was startled to see that it was surrounded by 'lots of little white things' which proved to be 'baby cockroaches. The adult was brooding and was very protective about getting the pale little animals under the protection of her wings.' Soon realizing that she as well as a number of other cockroach species were frequent visitors to, if not residents of, the outhouses that served the research camp, Kricher arranged field trips to the outhouses for his students. On one occasion, in Guatemala, he had them shine their flashlights down the holes where they could observe a veritable 'cockroach show . . . the students discussed long after returning home', some even claiming to have recurrent dreams about it, undoubtedly the impetus to future study – or significant contributions to the horror genre in which cockroaches so frequently star.[22]

Naturalist John Hay, walking in the 480,000 acre national park La Armitage in the Talamanca mountains of southern Costa Rica is completely appreciative of the impossible range of relationships and sizes among the area's insects: caterpillars 15 cm (6 inches) long and 'walking sticks of astonishing size, as well as giant grasshoppers, ants, and cockroaches in various

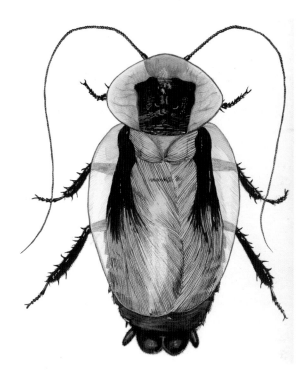

Called in Cuba the 'Cockroach of the Divine Face', the Central and South American *Blaberus giganteus* is a beautiful creature.

sizes'. To him their presence makes this one of nature's 'Sacred Places'.[23]

Perhaps because the cockroach is aware that some humans feel as Hay does, or because it is, in fact, uninterested in how we perceive it but is motivated by its own selfish needs, it has stuck by us wherever we have ventured. They are long time inhabitants of the Egyptian pyramids and accompanied us to the Arctic and Antarctic. The dusky cockroach has even colonized the homes of Laplanders, living off, among other Lap delicacies, dried fish. They have colonized the American Biosphere experiment in Arizona.

Most of the cockroach species purposely introduced to Biosphere 2 to simulate and balance the planet's various ecosystems failed to survive, suggesting we are still a long way from understanding how to 'manage' natural habitats as efficiently as nature does. However, representatives of the domestic species, undaunted by the fate of their wild cousins, continue to flourish in the Biosphere's living quarters with the human crew. Perhaps they simply like our company. Perhaps they intend to accompany us, when the time comes, to the far frontiers of space.

4 In the Mind of Man: Myth, Folklore and the Arts

Although the human chronicle explored in Chapter 3 is as filtered through the mind of modern man as any fictional account, knowledge of the shaping role of the imagination in myth and story makes many distrust the accuracy of what it records. Western literature has chronicled the cockroach – often quite accurately – since before Aesop and Aristophanes. As much literature as science deals with the poor creature's destruction: an Egyptian papyrus offers a prayer for protection from the cockroach and the classical Greek scholar Diophanes suggested fresh guts of rams, full of dung, would attract cockroaches. Burying the guts along with the cockroaches who had taken the bait for two days would effectively suffocate 'the Blats'.[1]

But not all literature cries out against the cockroach. Aesop's one cockroach character takes revenge on the eagle who killed his friend the hare, one of the few creatures willing to give the cockroach asylum. When the cockroach destroys the eagle's nest, the great bird puts her eggs in Zeus' lap for safe-keeping. The cockroach immediately flies up to Olympus and deposits dung on the god's lap, causing Zeus to leap up. In the process of brushing the cockroach droppings off, Zeus himself destroys the eagle's eggs.

Zeus and the eagle represent power and war and the fable – like Aristophanes' comedy *Peace* (422 BC) – speaks to the ability of the weak and despised to overcome them with a power older still. In *Peace*, the farmer Tygaeus determines to save his country from the ravages of the Peloponnesian War by scaling Olympus and freeing the goddess Peace from the grave in which the Olympians have buried her. The mount that carries the farmer to the heights is 'a man-sized cockroach he has brought home from Mt Etna', a place so famous from the fifth century on for its enormous cockroaches that they became symbols of the volcano and its chthonic powers – the forces of the dark magma and lava-rich core of the earth. We see here a yoking of opposites that occurs frequently in cockroach art, since the cockroach symbolizes both power and weakness, light and darkness in the same play. Perhaps the interplay of opposites suggests the degree to which Western humans struggle between the dualities imposed by our prevailing systems of philosophy and religion, a division that represses the secrets the cockroach persists in bringing to the surface.

Usually the cockroach appears in Greek satyr plays where, as in Attic comedy as a whole, allusions to its dung are primarily comic, but the roles of the cockroach in *Peace* and Aesop's fable are serious. Often indifferent to the fates of even his human characters, here Aristophanes is careful to assure the audience that Tygaeus' mount, like Pegasus himself, will live ever after in the stables on Olympus assured of a steady supply of food and destined to live forever, the ultimate survivor.[2]

The fate of the cockroach character in an Aesopian fable adapted for twenty-first century children by Paul Rosenthal is meant to be comic but instead reflects what has become the prevailing attitude toward cockroaches in contemporary Euro-American culture. In 'Cookie Crooks', a cat, a dog and a cockroach named Murray contrive to steal a bag of chocolate chip cookies stored high on the top of a cabinet. Neither cat nor dog can reach them, but Murray, although small and weak (Rosenthal retains the association of the cockroach with the weak that Aesop recognized), can. The bag is too big for him to push off, so the clever cockroach ties a string around it, dropping the end to the dog who pulls the bag down. While the dog and cat tear the bag open, Murray hurries back down to join the feast. The dog, his face full of crumbs, unapologetically stomps on the cockroach. Rosenthal's Aesopian moral emphasizes that although the strong are perfectly willing to exploit the weak, they are seldom happy to share the work, and never willing to share the prize.

Cockroaches, demonized and not, fill the imaginations of storytellers and artists worldwide. That distribution in turn suggests the cockroach is an archetypal image and, indeed, it is treated as such in the work of Jungian psychologist James Hillman. Joanne Luack points out that Joseph Campbell also recognizes in disgusting and rejected creatures like the cockroach the depths of the unconscious where we find the vision that wakes us from the familiar and outgrown into a new world.[3] Given the cockroach's predilection for the dark, it seems natural that Western cultures relegate it to the darkness we have come to associate with the unconscious and the power of the id, an association exploited to fine effect in Weiss's novel *The Roaches Have No King*.

Not so in other cultures: cultural entomologists have established that cockroaches, as well as other insects, frequently play roles ranging from trivial to cosmological in Native American mythology, especially in mythologies emerging from tropical areas. Navaho lore, for instance, equates them with the primordial beginnings of life.[4] Anthropologists and explorers note the relationships of a number of indigenous, traditional human cultures in Thailand, Australia, South America and French Guiana

to the cockroach, who appears both in their traditional medicines and their traditional tales as well as in their cuisine. What they reveal is that, rather than racking their brains for effective ways to destroy cockroaches, these cultures found the cockroach a useful neighbour, rich in protein and effective as medication for many human diseases. They also seem to have recognized how useful they were to the environment.

Zootherapeutic uses of the cockroach, many still current and treated as folk medicine by most modern practitioners, are found worldwide. Currently in northeastern Brazil and among practitioners of homeopathic medicine, dried cockroaches are used as a treatment for asthma. Interestingly, the one definitive relation between roaches and human disease is the role they play in hyperimmune (allergic and asthmatic) reactions. In *The Secret Life of Germs*, Philip M. Tierno concludes that poverty not the cockroach is 'the catalyst for the 158 per cent rise in asthma rates in the United States' over the past two decades. The rates of increase are highest by far among children in 'poor, dirty neighborhoods with high rates of infectious disease'.[5] Whatever allergens or diseases the cockroach carries, then, are the result of living in a contaminated environment. No cockroaches have been directly associated with particular disease cycles, as fleas, flies, ticks and mosquitoes have been – and cockroaches neither sting nor bite unless, in fact, they are eating.

Russian country folk still use powdered cockroach as a treatment for dropsy and, in other parts of Europe, cockroaches bruised, boiled, dried or fried in garlic oil are recommended for earache, weak sight, ulcers, dropsy, pleurisy, indigestion and pericarditis.[6] Australian Aborigines use them to obtain a local anaesthetic. The Roman author Pliny recommended crushed cockroach for itching, scabbing and ulcers, and ground cockroach fat, mixed with oil of roses, for earache. The latter, minus the roses and squeezed directly from the insect, is found in the folk medicines of southern African-Americans. Fried cockroach was used in African-American folk medicine to treat indigestion, and cockroach tea with a chaser of boiled cockroach poultice was believed to cure wounds and stingray burns.

Farther south, Jamaican Blacks 'drank the ashes of cockroaches as a tonic' and mixed 'bruised roaches, mixed with sugar' to encourage ulcers and tumours to burst.[7] In 'Quit Bugging Me! Suggestions for a Roach-Free Life', Julie Hughes notes that 'cockroaches have been used as cough syrup, to treat dropsy, irregular urination, poultices to reduce inflammation after being stung, and to cure indigestion'.[8]

Chinese medicine makes extensive use of insects and arthropods, the cockroach among them. Dried cockroaches are recommended for stroke victims and are readily available in markets in major cities. A fellow of the National Institute of Thai Traditional Medicine, Dr Kanvee Viwatpanich, has done extensive research on insect-based remedies, scouring ancient texts and consulting healers. As a result, he has come to believe the cockroach has the most medicinal potential of all insects. He encountered monks who fried a cockroach with pepper and seven centipedes, crushed them with honey, and used the concoction to treat sore throats. Another recommended remedy that the Institute is in the process of studying, this one for a sore often found on newborn babies, calls for a salve made of heated cockroach droppings.

In 2001 researchers at the Yunnan Medical College, motivated by the fact that an ethnic minority in Yunnan province in southwestern China has used cockroaches to cure open wounds, verified that a chemical compound extracted from cockroaches is effective in killing the AIDS virus.

The July 2002 issue of *Discover* announced that insect extract, cockroach extract among them, is the big hope of R&D, a biochemical company in Strasbourg, France. Since, as one of their biochemists puts it, 'Insects have evolved over 500 million years to survive in all kind of habitats,' it makes sense to assume they manufacture a wide range of biochemical defenses against threatening pathogens, some of which may be effective in combating human diseases. Perhaps it is time for the infamous Joe Skaggs to resurface with his 'Miracle Roach Hormone Cure' and reopen his museum of cockroach art and memorabilia!

Skaggs, self-described satirist, has for decades launched elaborate hoaxes aimed at revealing both the media's gullibility and the public's naïve acceptance of what it reads or sees. In 1981 he made a number of appearances on American talk shows and news broadcasts as Dr Josef Gregor, guru of a group called Metamorphosis, hawking a miracle drug made from cockroaches that guaranteed not only to cure whatever was wrong with you and to make you immune to radiation but also to ensure long-life. Orders poured in and folks eager to join Skaggs's group showed up to tour the Metamorphosis showroom and gallery.

Douglas A. Preston and Lincoln Child's thriller *The Cabinet of Curiosities* continues the adventures of Holmesian hero, FBI Special Agent Pendergast. In the 'grand subterranean cabinet of curiosities' of his great-grand-uncle – who had come from New Orleans where he had been influenced by voodoo practices, he discovers exhibit after exhibit of rare medicinal as well as poisonous insects, among them 'numberless cockroaches, from giant Madagascar hissing cockroaches to beautiful green Cuban roaches, winking in their jars like tiny emerald leaves' all 'collected because of the complex chemical compounds they contained'.[9]

In a short story, 'The Taste of Cockroach', the Australian Allan Baillie, whose assignments as a journalist have taken him to Southern Asia, narrates an exchange between two colonials in Laos in 1973 that introduces another universal role: the cockroach as food. The American traveller embraces the culture, urging his reluctant French companion to try 'a cooked and curried [cockroach] crescent'. When the Frenchman recoils, the American argues, 'But the Lao eat them like sweets . . . Have you ever tasted cockroach?' The American's *naïveté* is revealed when the other man explains that during the war he was isolated and starving in Laos, and survived by eating anything, even the abundant indigenous cockroaches.[10] David George Gordon points out that nautical scholars, also faced with starvation, found salted cockroaches tasty and nourishing and goes on to

The Cuban cockroach (*Panchlora nivea*), drawn here by Amy Bartlett Wright, frequently travels in bunches of bananas.

discuss how environmentally sound eating cockroaches is since it takes only a quarter as much feed to raise a pound of roach meat as it does to raise a pound of beef.

Actually, though it probably strikes Westerners as disgusting, cockroaches are eaten worldwide. Both columnist Dave Berry and the writer of 'Mean Cuisine'[11] note the close comparison, except in size, of the lobster and the cockroach. Indeed, as exterminator Gil Bloom puts it, the 'lobster is only a pair of antennae and a couple of feet away from being a cockroach'.[12] And, unlike its smaller, landlocked cousin, the lobster eats from the polluted sea bottom. If the common household cockroach is eaten, it must be purged in a secure container for several days on a diet of lettuce and apple since it, too, is likely

Cockroaches have long served as human food, as Brian Raszka's *Cockroaches on a Plate* reminds us.

to have consumed contaminated food. Wild cockroaches offer cleaner fare. Like lobsters, cockroaches are low in fat and high in protein.

Cockroaches are best when fresh, beheaded and delegged and then boiled, sautéed, grilled, dried or diced for sauces, as they are both in Thailand and Mexico. The New York Entomological Society is but one of a number of organizations that hold annual insect food festivals aimed at encouraging the general public to acquire a taste for nutritious, protein-rich insects like mealworms, grasshoppers and Thai waterbugs (cockroaches), which connoisseurs claim have the flavour of lettuce, seaweed or Gorgonzola cheese, depending on where you bite into it. At the National Pest Control festival in 1992, one *New Yorker* columnist tried to pin down the experts on whether the waterbug was the same insect as the American cockroach. One assured him it was – or a close relative anyway. Another with equal authority assured him that what they were eating was a true bug, while the roach was not a bug at all.

Most sources recommend not eating cockroaches raw. Nevertheless, like Dracula's cockroach-eating friend Renfield, a Scot plagued by several debilitating digestive problems has found that a diet of live Madagascar hissing roaches has completely cured his ills. According to a 2001 segment of *Ripley's Believe It or Not* TV show, he eats hundreds a day, prefers them fresh and active – as many prefer their clams and oysters live on the half-shell – and has had nary a moment's discomfort since they became his staple food.

But if you prefer your insects cooked, there are several excellent insect recipe books, such as Vincent M. Holt's 1885 *Why Not Eat Insects?*, Ronald Taylor and Barbara Carter's *Entertaining With Insects: The Original Guide to Insect Cookery* (1976; 1992), or David George Gordon's *The Eat a Bug Cookbook* (1998) which contains an intriguing recipe for cockroaches simmered in vinegar, sun-dried and then boiled with butter, farina, pepper and salt. A delectable recipe for Squatter's Pilaf that begins with collecting one hundred cockroaches is included in James Eckle's 'Road Kill, Road Eats'.[13]

A net search also provides cockroach recipes: the ultimate source is found at the Bay Area Bug Eating Society. Other net sources offer items cockroach-related in name only: Cockroach Clusters, for instance, are a candy made from chocolate, broken pretzels, and raisins; Chocolate Cockroaches appear in shops in Germany in spring when swarms of mating 'May beetles' can be seen everywhere; a Green Cockroach is a cocktail made of

Cockroach *hors d'œuvres*. Insect delicacies are arranged tastefully around a Thai waterbug, leaving little doubt of its relationship to the more familiar American cock-roach.

Tequila and Midori poured over ice and strained into an appropriate glass. However, a California firm, HOTLIX, creates an amber-like candy (Amber InsectNcides) as well as clear pops, both of which contain real home-grown edible insects, as well as a variety of chocolate covered bugs, cockroaches among them, albeit by special order.

Actually there is a potential unexplored market for cockroach goodies. Christopher S. Wren discovered, when assigned to the *New York Times'* Beijing office, that his cat Henrietta had an insatiable appetite for the crunchy critters that frequented the family's kitchen in impressive numbers. Not only did the cat prove as lethal to the population as any dedicated gecko, she also savoured her little treats as much as most humans savour salted nuts, thriving 'on fish cooked with rice and vegetables topped off with a savory . . . cockroach'.[14] Yet another flavour for the lucrative pet food market!

The truth is, given current practices of feeding animals destined for human consumption, we all probably consume more cockroaches than we know in our hamburgers and chops. And, actually, roach-infested grain or animal byproducts ground up into feed are probably the least dangerous of the substances permitted in the manufacture of stock feed. Undoubtedly a new folklore and literature revealing these facts will soon arise to join already established strands of cockroach lore.

One rich strand rose in Africa and, in 'a richly symbolic twist', since cockroaches accompanied them on the slave ships to the Americas, later in African-American folklore. Both traditions recognize and respect the cockroach as more than food or medicine. His tenacious hold on life makes him a survivor in many African and African-American tales. One tale from Antigua, 'The Cunning Cockroach', differs from tradition in that its Cockroach is not the survivor. It does, however, begin with an accurate bit of natural history: 'The cockroach can be a big creature, almost as big as your hand. You find cockroaches on the roof, where they make a noise like this: "Crum, crum, crum, crum, crum, crum!"' That established, the tale proceeds.

Two friends, Cockroach and Fowl, buy farmland together. Every day, when it is time to go to work the land, Cockroach would claim not to feel well and Fowl would go off alone. After Fowl was safely out of the way, Cockroach would jump up and spend the day singing and dancing. The song he sang – '*Cockroach a* cunnyman, *a* cunnyman, *a* cunnyman' – bragged about his cunning, a quality normally valued in African-American tales as necessary to outwit powerful masters. But here, when the cunning is directed toward a friend – one of

Cockroach's own – it is seen as a trait worthy of retribution and, indeed, Cockroach gets his comeuppance. A neighbour finally tells Fowl what is going on and the angry rooster 'came back and grabbed the cockroach, and he killed him. He swallowed him up that quick!'[15] There are many West Indian folk tales which, like this one, explain why chickens eat cockroaches with such vigour. The relationship may even be reflected in the common name *cock*roach – then again, the name may reflect other associations as well.

Early in his career the American writer Don Marquis served as an assistant editor under Joel Chandler Harris at the Atlanta *Constitution*. Harris, most famous for his adaptations of African-American folk tales in *Uncle Remus, His Songs and Sayings* (1880) and *Nights with Uncle Remus* (1895), encouraged Marquis's interests in folklore and fantasy. Although Marquis wrote novels, plays and poems, he is best known for his cockroach poet and amanuensis, archy. The links between archy and African American folklore, as well as the fantasy tradition of talking animals, explain at least in part why the cockroach continues to figure in contemporary folk tradition as the survivor who sees life from the underside and 'tells it like it is'. It also, in the modern context, makes archy a champion of both human and nonhuman underdogs and, indeed, the predominant tone in his voice is irony and satire, comedy but comedy with dark undertones.

In 'archy declares war', enraged by having seen a kitchen worker poisoning 'water bugs,' and thinking

of all
the massacres and slaughter
of persecuted insects
at the hands of cruel humans

he finds himself crying 'aloud to heaven' and kneels

> on all six legs
> and vowed a vow
> of vengeance[16]

as many a slave over the centuries must have done; although most of their folktales, for obvious reasons, sublimate the anger carefully.

The African roots of these tales is supported by the appearance, not only of the cockroach as either character or symbol in many works of African art and literature, but in the use of a proverb related to another African-American tale of the Cockroach and Fowl as the epigram for Tchicaya U Tam'si's Congolese novel *Les Cancrelats*: '*Le cancrelat alla plaider une cause du tribunal des poules*' ('The Cockroaches: The cockroach went to plead its cause before the hens'). Both the proverb and the image of the cockroach reappear at significant points in the first and the last (*Les ptealenes*) of the trilogy that encompasses the author's sociopolitical fresco of the Congo.[17]

The symbolic significance of the cockroach moved South African artist Walter Oltmann to create a copper-wire sculpture of a local cockroach, the Parktown Prawn, a nocturnal scavenger considered grotesque by the owners of the Highvelt gardens it populates. This large cockroach struck the artist as a perfect vehicle to represent the tensions or ambivalences between public and private, past and present, wild and domestic. He comments that 'By weaving such an insect in copper wire on a scale close to that of a human baby, I . . . invest it with a sense of intimacy and pathos. The copper wire lends itself ideally to capturing the colour and richness of surface detail of the insect and by depicting it as a dead, limp body, I wanted to create an image that would be disquietingly beautiful and

Libanasidus vittatus (copper-wire cockroach), a sculpture by Walter Oltmann.

charged with the ambivalence of being both repulsive and attractive'.[18]

An African-American tale, with variants from Antigua and Surinam, about Cockroach and the spider trickster Anansi, can be read as a cautionary tale. Anansi, also brought with slaves from Africa, became a common figure in African American folklore. As early as 1815 Matthew Gregory Lewis, author of the Gothic novel *The Monk*, who had inherited an estate in Jamaica, where it is rumoured that spiders were kept in houses to keep them cockroach free, recorded in his Journal that there were tales he calls 'Nancy stories' (also Aunt Nancy stories) prevalent among his slaves. They suggested the value of being a trickster if one were to survive oppression.

In the United States, Anansi eventually metamorphosed into the figure of Brer Rabbit made familiar by Joel Chandler Harris, but in the Caribbean, he stayed his original spider self as he does in the tale in question. In it, Anansi challenges Cockroach to a climbing contest, betting he could reach the top of the tree first. Cockroach, guessing rightly that Anansi had forgotten cockroaches have wings, takes the bet. When the trickster reaches the top of the tree, he finds Cockroach already there. Of course he contests the outcome, claiming flying had not been included in the original wager. Since the two cannot

Originally from equatorial Africa, the American cockroach (*Periplaneta americana*) prefers the warm, moist ambiance of sewers and wharfs.

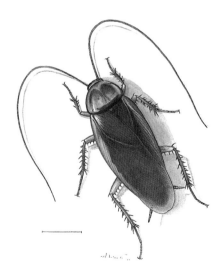

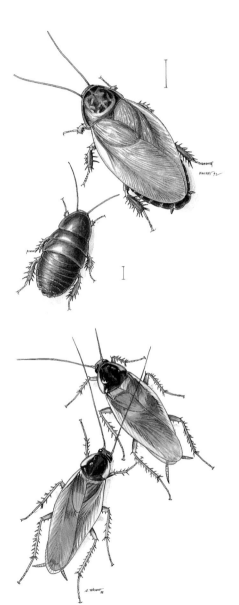

Surinam cockroach (*Pycnoscelus surinamensis*). Over 200 years after Maria Sibylla Merian first painted this species, Amy Bartlett Wright chooses the same subject.

Brown-banded cockroach (*Supella longipalpa*) by Amy Bartlett Wright. In females the wing covers are shorter than in males, revealing a fetching view of their abdomens.

settle their dispute, they decide to find a judge, and who do they call in but Fowlcock?

After considering the case, he crows and calls the two over, eating Cockroach up as soon as he is near enough. End of dispute! Of course, it warns listeners to trust no one, especially judges like the Cock. Not surprisingly, a Caribbean proverb strikingly similar to the one used in U Tam'si's novel *Les Cancrelats*, suggests '*Ravet pas ni raison duvan pul*' ('Cockroach has no rights before fowl'). The inclusion of cockroaches in commercial chicken feed testifies to the accuracy of both these traditions. The wild relatives of our hens and roosters are natural predators of the wild cockroach.

There is some evidence of a similar tradition in European folklore. Since the spread of the pest species, the company of the domestic cockroach, whether American, German, Oriental, Surinam or Brown-banded, has seldom been appreciated and has often been demonized. Remnants of older folk traditions, however, recall a long-ago positive relationship in Europe. It was once customary to release cockroaches in new buildings in Europe because they were thought to be lucky and treated as honoured guests. One Hungarian folk song (set to music by Bartok and called 'New Hungarian Folk Song') tells, not of the wedding of Martina and the mouse, but of the cricket and the spider's daughter. The bride is attended by 'gnats and fleas' and the 'Cockroach wants to be best man.' 'Is that such a bad thing?' asks the chorus. Though the question isn't answered, the implication is that, considering that the affair is to be a 'Creepy crawly mad fling!', he would make an appropriate attendant for the groom.[19]

One persistent south-of-the border tale, apparently intended to teach youngsters values, involves a vain adolescent female cockroach, usually called Martina. There are a number

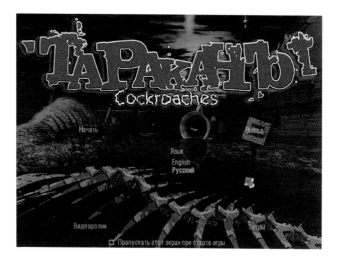

The garish colours of this Russian arcade game provide a fitting accompaniment for Victor Pelevin's *The Life of Insects* somewhat allegorical vision of contemporary Russia from the perspective of its insect population.

of versions, some bilingual, currently in print like 'La Cucaracha Martina y el Ratincito' ('The Little Cockroach Martina and the Little Rat') that are widely used in European and American classrooms. This tale has a parallel in Indian folklore. In the *pourquois* folktale collected by Anne Sinclair Mehdevi in *Persian Folk Tales*, 'Mistress Cockroach', a lady cockroach, dressed in her wedding finery, begins to put on airs and rejects a number of cockroach suitors because they will not promise to pamper her after they marry. Finally she accepts a mouse who, indeed, treats her like a queen. When he dies, she swears never to wear finery again, adopting the drab colours domestic cockroaches wear to this day.

Usually Russian and Hungarian writers replace the positive emphasis placed on the cockroach by writers from the underside with a more negative one although Victor Pelevin's *The Life of Insects* employs a host of insect characters, good and bad, including cockroaches, to satirize post-soviet Russia. But in

A civilizator ('The Civilizer') by the Hungarian playwright Imre Madach, the cockroach police, able to penetrate any crack and dig into any dirt, serve Stroom, the German 'civilizer' rather than the Hungarians. Interestingly, the word for cockroach in Hungarian, *svabbogar* or *svab*, actually means Swabian bug, Swabian being a generic term for German-speaking settlers.[20] The Russian Chukovskii Konnshevich's *Tarakanshye* ('The Cockroach'), a rare children's book, contains a despotic cockroach who terrorizes other animals until he is eaten by a bird.

A far less ominous Finnish tale tells of the origin of the cockroach as does a tale from India, which includes a magic whistle that brought the first cockroach to life. Another Indian tale explains how cockroaches came from the wild to share the homes of humans. In 1996, Norma J. Livo included a cockroach tale she had discovered in *Donegal Fairy Tales* (1900) in her *Troubadour's Storybag*. Although the connection seems tenuous, the tale of 'The Bee, the Mouse, and the Bum-Cock' certainly suggests the presence of the cockroach – the Bum-Cock is, according to Philip Smith, editor of *Irish Fairytales* (1993), a cockroach – in Celtic folklore. And there is no question about the respect paid the cockroach by the Neapolitan folk saying Schweid uses to preface his book and Maxine Kumin to preface her 2002 poem

'The Fable of the Cockroach and the Housewife' illustrates the age-old affinity between cockroach and housewife.

on the cockroach ('The Survivor'): 'Every cockroach is beautiful to its mother!'

Nonetheless, in European and American folklore the war between the cockroach and the housewife has become almost as pervasive as has the cockroach/fowl association in African and African-American folklore. Entomologist Howard Ensign Evans suggests, as may well be the case, that the housewife lore may have had its genesis in the earliest of man's dwellings. Even fossil cockroaches, 249 million years the housewife's senior, 'look so much like contemporary species', he writes, 'that one can almost imagine them freshly crushed by some irate housewife'.[21]

In work after work of literature, Tawfig al-Hakim's 'The Fate of a Cockroach' and William Gass's 'Order of Insects' to name a notable two and Stephen Raleigh Byler's 'Roaches', in *Searching for Intruders:A Novel in Stories* (2002), the most recent, the cockroach proves a threat to the housewife's sense of propriety and duty whether in Cairo or the American heartland or New York City. Contemporary essayist Sarah Scalet, herself a New York City housewife, writes:

When I saw the first cockroach in my kitchen, it took me less than 10 seconds to metamorphose from a nonviolent nature lover into a coldhearted killer. So much for my chemical-free garden . . . So much for the renegade moths I captured . . . and released outdoors . . . So much for vegetarianism, organic foods, and my skepticism of dry-cleaning chemicals. Logic cannot explain the shiver I felt in my spine, the primal desire I had to kill that cockroach *dead*.[22]

Sue Hubbell, who, in *A Country Year*, explains that neither the

Cockroaches living in little homes reminiscent of the world of Beatrix Potter and other illustrators. From Catherine Chalmers's roach series *Infestation*.

These *Kitchen Door Panels* show, rather than flowers and fruit, household pests. Designed by Sheena See.

wood cockroaches in her woodpile nor the cockroaches that seek to help themselves to the goodies to be found in her beehives require her intervention. A healthy beehive deals with invaders by itself and, since wood-roaches do not share 'an ecological niche' with her, she finds no need 'to squish them as a housewife would'.[23] Scalet too came to her senses, recognizing that ironically the German cockroaches in her Boston apartment were 'the closest thing to wildlife' in the neighbourhood.

The rich mélange of themes associated with the cockroach in literature and lore helps to explain why cockroaches abound worldwide in contemporary pop culture (in music, on stamps, in movies, in collectables and comics) as well. Internet sites and tourist shops offer a veritable bonanza of cockroach collectables from expensive toys like the Folkman's Puppet Cockroach

Peg McDonald using the Folkmann cockroach puppet to convey 'her love of crawly creatures' to children.

Pocket Pests™. Numerous versions of such creatures exist to be used in practical – and not so practical jokes.

A 'Colorful Cockroach Costume' designed by Encore Playstation, Singapore, for a customer in China.

Allpet Roaches

O.McMonigle
R.Willis

Care and Identification
Handbook for the Pet and
Feeder Cockroaches

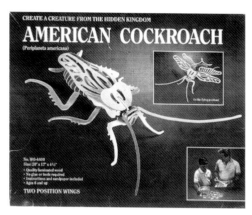

CREATE A CREATURE FROM THE HIDDEN KINGDOM

AMERICAN COCKROACH
(*Periplaneta americana*)

No. WO-4400
Size: 20" x 17" x 4½"
• Quality laminated wood
• No glue or tools required
• Instructions and sandpaper included
• Ages 6 and up

TWO POSITION WINGS

and Marie Osmond's Count Cocky Cockroach doll, part of her Beauty Bug Ball™ collection, and fine jewellery and art as well as the kind of art sold at the Combat Cockroach Hall of Fame in Plano, Texas,[24] which sponsors a contest to encourage people to kill cockroaches and then dress and pose them as humans in shoebox scenes. There are cheap plastic and rubber cockroaches – Pocket Pests™ – intended to startle the squeamish. There are elaborate and colourful cockroach costumes and, of course, there are those who collect living cockroaches – or keep them as pets – as well, and therefore markets for pet and exotic cockroaches like Allpet Roaches. There are cockroach lunch boxes, cameras, ceramic tiles, blocks, toys and models, and tee- and sweatshirts both serious and vile. There are cockroach greeting cards and postcards. There is even a cosmetics company, Urban Decay™, which markets such shades as 'Gosh' and 'Cockroach' to human nymphs who desire unusual colours.

Allpet Roaches is a useful booklet that recounts the history and lore of the cockroach, and offers advise about pet-keeping.

The American cockroach (*Periplaneta Americana*) is part of a series of models, 'The Hidden Kingdom of the Insect World'.

'I got over
DDT . . .' (1993)
by Leo Cullum.

"*I got over DDT, and I'll get over you!*"

Although popular culture is in many ways the folk tradition of the late twentieth and early twenty-first centuries, nothing comes closer to representing our time than its popular music (except perhaps its comics and comic strips which require a picture gallery to appreciate as befits their visual nature). In both the cockroach figures large. A friend downloading cockroach music from the Internet filled two CD-Roms with currently popular cockroach songs and musical arrangements and then found his cockroach files heavily pirated. In addition to 'La Cucaracha', which every American schoolchild learns to sing in grade school, one German punk rock group calls itself The Cockroach, and a Scandinavian group is called the Cockroach Clan. The American Roches is an all-female *a cappella* group from the San Francisco Bay Area,[25] and Papa Roach, whose first release, *Infest* (2000), was full of 'meat-pounder riffs', is influential 'rap-metal grudge-rock' that spawned the current nu-metal sound of garage rock.[26]

A recent and popular comic book, China's *Cockroach* is making an impact both at home and in Europe.

Music groups Papa Roach and the Osbournes, illustration by Hungry Dog Studios for *Entertainment Weekly* (2000).

While the cockroach has had less impact on classical composers and performers, attention must be paid to the libretto Marc Abrahams and Don Kates produced for the sixth annual Ig Nobel Prize Ceremony in 1996. 'Lament del Cockroach: a mini-opera for Nobel Laureates and mezzo-sopranos' features the tragic demise of Thelma Roach who succumbs to bacteria brought to earth by a meteorite from Mars accompanied by music adapted from Wagner. Survivors greet the death of the last cockroach (and of the myth of cockroach survival) with the triumphal music of Handel's 'Hallelujah Chorus'.

Finally, there is the suggestive tale told in Australian author Trevor Todd's young adult novel, *The Cockroach that Wrote a Symphony*. Teenager Benjy, reluctantly missing outdoor fun with his friends because his music homework is not finished, is startled when a cockroach darts across his desk. About to slam a book on it, he notices something unbelievable – the cockroach is writing a line of music on Benji's lesson staff. Not unlike Marquis's archy, this cockroach laboriously gathers a blob of ink at a time with his front legs, then scampers back and forth, shaping note after note. Taking what the cockroach had finished to his music teacher without telling her its source, Benjy and his mother listen entranced as the 'strong opening chords, and then a beautiful melody . . . flowed over them'.[27]

Once Miss Bell learns who is writing the music, she approaches a famous conductor who is impressed enough to visit Benjy's house to see the cockroach composer for himself. Determined to perform the Cockroach Symphony with the National Symphony Orchestra, Sir Peregrin issues a press release. That very night Benjy returns home to find that, just as in Kafka's *Metamorphosis*, the cleaning lady has crushed the cockroach and thrown him in the dustbin. Although Benjy is thrilled when Sir Peregrin finishes and performs the cockroach's symphony, its success fails to compensate for the loss of his friend's company.

The intriguing question, given the many positive associations with the cockroach found in folklore, literature and popular culture is why the cockroach remains the least-loved of all creatures, lowest among the low. On the other hand, it is exactly this ambiguity that sets the cockroach up as satire's darling, and allows it to continue to question boundaries and set question marks after certainties – exactly what marks the cockroach as the totem animal of all those humans also relegated to the undersides of their cultures despite their virtues and gifts.

5 Tales from the Underside

Although species distribution tells us that the association is inaccurate, cockroaches have become synonymous with urban environments. Nothing catches this attitude more forcefully than the 1997 horror thriller *Mimic* in which New York City's underside, literally infested with cockroaches, is turned into a vast cockroach nest where mutant creatures breed and wreak vengeance on those above. Most of the contemporary musical groups and musicians who have sought identification with the cockroach see themselves, like the cockroach, as belonging to the underside, certainly outside of, mainstream society. For them the pest species of cockroach provide a fitting totem and, in fact, there are far fewer 'pest species' of cockroach than counter-culture musical groups flourishing in our cities.

One of the street gangs made famous by Martin Scorsese's 2002 film, *Gangs of New York*, is the Roach Guards of Mulberry Street. Although actually named for the greengrocer whose establishment served as the gang's headquarters, its participation in the raw life of the early nineteenth-century scramble for survival in the urban jungle makes it impossible not to associate the gang with the cockroach. The Roach Gang may even be responsible for the use of the shortened term 'roach' for the insect, which began in New York in this period. Adam Gopnik's *New Yorker* review of the 2003 edition of Herbert Ashby's study,

Twilight of the Cockroaches (1987) by Hiroaki Yosida sides with the cockroach as urban humans try to exterminate them.

on which Scorsese based his film, carries the association with the cockroach further when he refers to the film's Jake La Matta as a 'cockroach'[1] As May Berenbaum puts it, these 'few bad apples' have tainted the whole cockroach tribe as far as most humans are concerned.

Charles Simic, who describes himself as a poet of the city in a 1984 interview, claims the rat as his totem animal and the cockroach as his muse exactly because these two creatures seem synonymous with the urban scene. The cockroach is equally a symbol for drug culture (butts of joints are called 'roaches' and are held in 'roachclips'), the criminal, the immigrant – an advertisement 'For Combat Roach Bait shows a bunch of dead cockroaches lying on their backs with the caption "Tired of living with thousands of strangers" – a clear appeal to resentment against recent immigrants'.[2] When mob boss John Gotti received a life sentence in 1992, a *New York Times* article reported that he had referred to the snitch responsible for his conviction as 'a cockroach', implying not only that he was the lowest of low but also that 'he could be eliminated as easily as squashing a bug'.[3]

For related reasons, cockroaches constitute predictable allusions on American TV series such as *Law & Order*, which is set in New York City, when victims or suspects reside in one of the city's ethnic neighborhoods. A typical exchange involved a young Puerto Rican woman whose sister had been raped and beaten by an enemy of her drug-dealing boyfriend. When cornered by Brisco, a detective who accuses her of luring her sister into a trap which, like a cockroach motel, had no exits, she responds, 'And cockroaches deserve to die?' Another episode shows Brisco urging the arrest of a Latino suspect 'before he scuttles away and hides with all the other cockroaches'.

Cockroaches can also symbolize the working class, as is suggested by Robert Malecki's *Cockroach! An EZINE for Poor and Working Class People*. Philip Paul Hallie recollects that his Chicago boyhood was spent in a building aptly named 'the Cockroach building' on Roosevelt Road near Kedzie. Frank Waters summarizes the roach's urban associations in his 1947 novel *The Yogi of Cockroach Court*, set in a Mexican border town in the United States where 'the unfortunates, *putas* and *pajaritas* . . . were known as cockroaches' and are segregated in Cockroach Court. Waters omits at least one maligned group, as mystery writer Shirley Rousseau Murphy has her cat detective Joe Gray point out in *Cat Spitting Mad*: he 'knew of dog-oriented families where cats came under the heading of vermin – right down there with a cockroach in the kitchen cupboard'.[4] Usually, the link is reserved for humans ostracized for whatever reason from the mainstream culture, an association evoked by Chicano writer Oscar Zeda Acosta when he titled his expose of the urban underside *The Revolt of the Cockroach People* (1973).

Cockroaches make frequent appearances in works by Latino-Americans and, in 'mainstream' culture, are frequently associated with them (as we have seen in episodes of *Law & Order*). Puerto Rican poet Pedro Pietri in 'Suicide Note from a Cockroach in a Low Income Housing Development', allows his cockroach narrator to make a long, heart-rending complaint, which is, without much adjustment, as applicable to the lives of the humans living confined to urban slums as to roaches. His metaphors are strong – full of genocide and despair. He urges his human readers to answer his charges, forwarding his 'mail to your conscience when you get one'.[5] Among Latino Americans, the cockroach, echoing the dichotomy between weak and strong found in Aristophanes' *Peace*, is also often associated positively with rebellion as it is in both Acosta and in Martin Espada's poem 'Cockroaches of Liberation'. Espada's activist students are equated with cockroaches, 'multiplying in the dark,' who 'strike and disappear, ' 'too quick for stomping boots'.[6]

Hispanic novelist Junot Diaz's debut collection, *Drown* (1996), links the lives of his characters with the presence of cockroaches in apartments in Washington Heights and the Bronx and near-by Edison, New Jersey. More common is the association of the cockroach with the hopelessness and squalor of the urban slum, an association found, for instance, in Cherrie Moraga's theatre piece 'The Shrunken Head of Pancho Villa'. Her 1950s California barrio becomes shabbier and shabbier as the play progresses, its degeneration represented by the red cockroaches first dotting and finally totally covering its walls.

Latino novelist Sandra Cisnernos creates an exterminator character, Flavio Munguia, proud proprietor of La Cucaracha Apachurrada ('The Squished Cockroach') in *Bien Pretty*. He represents, according to critic Harryette Mullen, 'the indigenous creativity and cultural authenticity of the barrio'. William S. Burroughs's urban novels *Exterminator!* and *The Naked Lunch* are also urban cockroach chronicles, as are the films they inspired. In fact, director David Cronenberg, who made both films, has become one of our premier cockroach chroniclers.

The National Geographic Society's documentary *Doctor Cockroach*, based on the life of real-life exterminator Astin Frishman, was perhaps the first cockroach film that required the services of a roach wrangler, a position that received a good deal of media attention when feature films like *Joe's Apartment* and *Mimic* were being filmed. Interestingly their job includes both the managing and the welfare of the film's cockroach characters.

The hero of satiric novelist Bill Fitzhugh's *Pest Control* (1996), an exterminator rather than a roach wrangler, is none the less concerned with the welfare of insects, humans, and the environment they share. Fitzhugh's research for the novel earned him a contract in 1993 to write the insect episode of PBS's 'Eyewitness' series, co-produced by the BBC, a production that benefited from the same meticulous research that makes the insects in *Pest Control* so successful. In a recent email, Fitzhugh described both as 'half natural history and half about the cultural influence of insects'.

The novel's exterminator character, Bob, quite unlike any Burroughs' character, is the essential American innocent, passionately dedicated to ridding the world of the contaminating effects of DDT and more recent potent toxins used to control insects by replacing them with a biological control he is developing – his Assassin Beetles. Specially bred to kill and eat pest species like the cockroach, they are a vivid presence in the novel.

The Liverpool *Daily Post* claimed that Bill Fitzhugh's novel 'does for beetles what *Jurassic Park* did for dinosaurs'.

His cockroaches are victims and pretty benign beings until they manage to interbreed with one of Bob's hybrids. Then, like Bob, the cockroaches become – albeit mistakenly – assassins themselves, condemned to the underside of the city by those in control.

New York City can probably claim the title of roach capital of the world: the New York Police Department has a full-time entomologist to determine whether wounds on the city's murder victims were caused by human violence or hungry cockroaches or both. In the late 1970s Eugene J. McCarthy recognized the association in 'Roaches Take Over New York City Buses', explaining

> . . . there is roaches' work to be done on buses.
> Removing crumbs,
> Keeping the engines clean of grease.
> . . .

Cockroaches as victims of human forms of execution, in a series of photographs – *Executions* – by Catherine Chalmers.

Roaches go where they are needed.
And as a spokesman for the Transit Co. said,
'It's not a problem unique to buses.
Once a roach settles in, he's as much at home
On a city bus as in a Park Avenue apartment.'[7]

Or, as Patricia Highsmith observes in 'Noted From a Respectable Cockroach', they are at home in New York's finest hotels.

In a recent review of Highsmith's stories, Margo Jefferson notes: 'Kafka's Gregor Samsa is human and tragic; Don Marquis's archy is a gentle humanist. Highsmith's cockroach is a snob with an ancient lineage and no name – he has too much disdain for bipeds to want or need one.'[8] Her disgruntled protagonist moves out of the Hotel Duke on Washington Square in the suitcase of an equally distraught British tourist because the clientele had become so 'un-Henry Jamesian' and the building so degenerate.

Among New York's literary cockroaches, Don Marquis's archy, shaking off his folkloric roots, becomes the quintessential benign urban cockroach. However, the far-from-gentle roach protagonists of Daniel Weiss's *The Roaches Have No King* are equally New York roaches.[9] In this novel the sexual associations of the cockroach are more graphically displayed than in any other work, suggesting why particularly Freudian analysts like Camille Paglia have seen the cockroach as symbol not just of the underside but also of the dark and sexual powers of the id. In *Sexual Personae: Art and Decadence from Nefertiti to Emily Dickinson* (1991), she claims that nineteenth-century Romanticism refocused the modern male's imagination, reconnecting him with the prehistoric female earth powers long dominated by anthropocentric male hierarchy, a path she believes led directly to Kafka's Gregor Samsa. Perhaps this is why, ultimately, we will

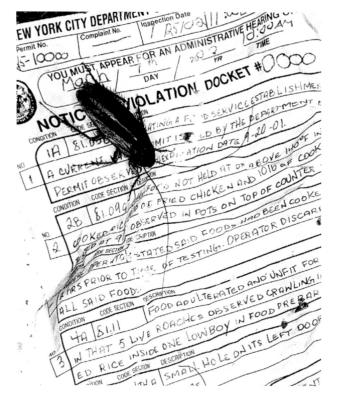

Violation Docket #0000.
Ruven Afandor's illustration for Elizabeth Kolbert's *New Yorker* article, 'Everyone Lies: Making the Rounds With Restaurant Inspectors' (19 & 26 August 2002), suggests how strongly roaches are associated with urban eating establishments. Cockroaches are not mentioned in the article.

find Kafka's Gregor leading us toward an ecofeminist vision firmly rooted in the fertile soil of the chthonic or earthly powers.

Another scene in Weiss's novel, exploring another realm of Freudian association, uses a flush toilet as a magic portal through which narrator and main cockroach character, Numbers, leads the readers on a tour of New York's dark and 'vast network of impregnable tunnels' far more graphic than the sewer scenes in the film *Mimic*. Perhaps the only account more vivid than either *Mimic*'s or Weiss's comes from Brian M. Wiprud, Inspector for the City of New York. In his essay 'Ratville' Wiprud describes an infestation of mutant white leviathans that he discovered on the sides of an old brick manhole at a midtown intersection that boasts restaurants on every corner:

> When the lid came off, nothing seemed amiss, but when the sun began to penetrate the darkness, the crew noticed something odd . . . It was the cumulative aura radiating from 100,000 insects . . . when the crane dropped the lid, the jolt started a stampede. Completely carpeted with 'water bugs,' the walls surged outward. A blanket of roaches spread from the hole like a death shadow, jolting a spasm

A scene from Robert Crumb's comic book version (1995) of Franz Kafka's classic tale, *Metamorphosis*.

THE METAMORPHOSIS

"The pain was shocking, unbelievable. The last thing Gregor saw before he passed out was his mother rushing to his father, begging him to spare her son's life."

A month passed. Lame from his injury, the apple festering in his back, Gregor was now "covered in dust; hair and bits of old food stuck to his back and sides, and trailed after him. . . ." His beloved sister no longer bothered to clean his room.

New Yorker
Gregor Cartoons:
Catering to its
literary-minded
readers, *The New
Yorker* has
published several
Gregor-associated
cartoons, notable
among them
Robert Searle's
'Lewis Carroll
Meets Kafka' and
– seen here –
Eldon Dedini's
Gregor Samsa III,
who doesn't get
out much.

*Gregor Samsa III, who doesn't go out much, calls in a
large order to the shopping channel.*

of panic in onlookers. Civilians literally screamed, running
for the nearest open doorway and scrambling onto car
hoods. Workers cursed, jumping onto excavators and lamp
posts like elephants fleeing mice. And I don't need to tell
you where the roaches disappeared. While many funneled
down catch basins back into the sewer, a huge number
seized the opportunity and made for the restaurants,
fluidly slipping under the doors by the thousands.[10]

Perhaps even more disturbing because more personally
invasive, poet C. K. Williams describes an infestation of a New

The popular CD-Rom game *Bad Mojo* (Pulse), issued in 1996, encourages its human player to think like a roach.

York City apartment house so intractable that insecticides prove useless. An elderly neighbour who had 'gone through deportation/and the camps' and now is close to death, is found, wedged 'between his toilet and a wall', his skin alive with cockroaches who are undaunted by either light or the 'Samaritan neighbor' who scraped them off the old man's 'barely breathing' body.[11]

Despite their less 'insolent, impervious' demeanours, Marquis's archy and Kafka's Gregor Samsa have proved even more prolific and memorable than such real-life models. Each has spawned a multitude of offspring, most equally urban.

118

Kafka's *Metamorphosis* is set in Prague in the early twentieth century and is deeply urban. While archy often stands up for the downtrodden, nothing in Marquis matches Kafka's evocation of the dehumanizing effect of modern society. Understandably this is a theme frequently echoed in other modern and postmodern writers.

Among Gregor's progeny are some of the writings of Nobel-prize-winner Gabriel García Márquez, who pointed to 'The Metamorphosis' as the catalyst for his own writing career in an 1988 interview in *El Pais*. Quoting the memorable first line of the story verbatim, he claims the story made him think 'Damn! . . . if you can do this . . . then I can do it! . . . This is how my

The movie *Joe's Apartment* (1996) includes appealing musical comedy numbers.

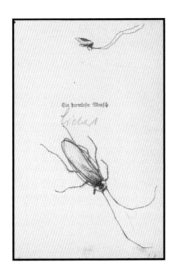

Gregor, part of a 1995 triptych by Todd Somerville, refers to plagues and other topics and their effect on human culture.

grandfather told stories . . . The most unusual things, with the greatest naturalness.'[12] Thus Kafka's giant insect emerges early as the father of magic realism, a connection that has been overlooked by a number of mainstream commentators who have assumed that Gregor is to be understood as a symbol rather than as animals are in the traditions of magic realist writing.

For them, Gregor is a symbol of either society or of the human Gregor's psychological response to his situation. In *Countries of the Mind*, for instance, Gillian Tindall comments that after the appearance of Kafka's *Metamorphosis*, the roach becomes a symbol of 'the claustrophobic bourgeoisie interior . . . a classic symbol for crushed emotion . . . frustration, repression, and womb-like regression' and its accompanying separation from the natural world experienced by the middle class in both Europe and the United States.[13]

Without denying the relevance of such an interpretation, a number of critics, Walter Benjamin, John Gardner, Harold

Blackham and Kafka's translator Jay Neugreshel among them, have insisted that Kafka intended his audience to respond to his many animal characters as what they are, in this case a giant insect (possibly a cockroach). They suggest that like Márquez, Kafka creates empathy – total mental and spiritual identification' – for nonhuman characters in the readers of his animal fictions.

Works that bring the most biologically and emotionally accurate cockroach characters to life follow in this tradition, not unrelated to the animistic aura of magic realism. Often they view the cockroach as a positive creature as they appear in first the MTV popular short spot 'Joe's Apartment' and then in the delightful but not as successful feature film musical of the same name. The most recent works to continue this tradition are Marc Estrin's novel *Insect Dreams: The Half-Life of Gregor Samsa* (2002) and Reza Ordoubadian's 'Kafka's Cockroach,' a short story of some length.[14] Both bring Kafka's Gregor, a human-sized cockroach, but one who survived his family's neglect, from Prague to New York. In both he is Jewish. Ordoubadian's Gregor suffers the Holocaust in Prague before leaving Europe for the United States; the European experience comprises the most significant portion of the story. In Estrin's version, the heart of the novel lies in the United States, first in New York in the 1920s. Because he is Jewish, rather than because he is a cockroach, 'Estrin's Gregor lived in the *Unterwelt*, an "underworld" not in the Plutonic sense, but in the way the "underdog" is under.'[15] Both cockroach and Jew are treated by the average New Yorker as vermin, much as Estrin's Gregor was treated by the German audience when he was in Hoffnung's Cabinet of Wonders in Vienna at the turn of the century.

This theme is picked up again when Estrin's Gregor serves in the Roosevelt administration during World War II's Holocaust.

The illustrations by George Harriman for Don Marquis's classic have become universally recognized.

There his ideas are referred to as 'the Jewish cockroach view' and Gregor acknowledges that

> Jews are cockroaches, in a way. They must become hard on the outside from so much kicking around. But they are soft on the inside ... Like cockroaches Jews represent everything not to be digested, everything otherness, everything getting in the way, everything that will not be expelled – just like other poor people, Orientals, Negroes

HI-HI
HEH
HEH
HEH
HI!!

HAW
HAW
HAW

HORSE
SHAKESPEARE
& I .

HERRIMAN.

Here Harriman's archy enjoys an evening with a familiar fellow poet and dramatist at the Mermaid Tavern, London.

– like cockroaches. We always reopen the wound of all-not-accomplished-by-society. So we are fit for only one thing: extermination.[16]

Estrin's Gregor is only one of many literary descendants of Kafka's Gregor. Jan Krupinski, the human protagonist of Polish-American playwright Janus Glowacki's 'Hunting Cockroaches', refers to Gregor as 'The hero of Kafka's *Metamorphosis*. The one who was transformed into a cockroach.'[17] His lower Eastside New York City slum apartment, where the immigrant Krupinskis, respected professionals in their old country, are forced to live is filled with cockroaches. The lives of the apartment's human and cockroach denizens are equated with the failure of the country to welcome and value immigrants to its shores.

Kit Reed's 1968 short story 'Sisohpromatem' is, like its title, a reversal of Kafka's formula: Joseph Bug woke one morning to

find himself an enormous human. Similarly, in Mary James's young adult novels *Shoebag* (1990) and *Shoebag Returns* (1998), a young cockroach wakes one morning to find he has turned into a human boy. Shunned by his family and friends because as a human he is seen as both monstrous and 'bacteria-laden', Stuart Bagg acquires a champion named Samsa at the local elementary school. In the sequel, at Miss Rattray's School for Girls, Stuart (undoubtedly named for E. B. White's *Stuart Little*) champions the misfits who are rejected by the school's elite. In fact *The School Library Journal* referred to James's novels as 'a multi-layered experience', which allows young readers to experience 'the absurdity of prejudice', a theme never far from the core of cockroach literature.[18] Jane Smiley's 'Gregor: My Life as a Bug', first

Ralph Lee's puppetry adaptation, *Communications from a Cockroach: archy and the underside* (2001), was presented in New York City's parks.

Martha Paulos's illustration of the pantry shelf that is the setting for Christopher Morley's poem 'To a Cockroach'.

published in *Harper's* in 1992, puts an ecofeminist twist on Kafka's tale. Nor is Gregor's influence limited to literature. In 1978, the Canadian animated cartoonist Carolyn Leaf produced *The Metamorphosis of Mr Samsa*.

Archy's creator, Don Marquis – Donald Robert Perry Marquis (1878–1937) – first introduced his cockroach poet in his *New York Sun* column in 1913. The little fellow, the reincarnation of a *vers libre* poet, created his verses by leaping onto the keys of Marquis's typewriter when the columnist's office was deserted at night. He uses neither capital letters nor punctuation because he cannot work the shift key. His wise and cynical commentary on life, insect, feline (mehitabel is archy's unforgettable alley-cat pal), and human, proved so popular that Marquis, a widely published novelist and playwright, came to fear his fame would ultimately rest on a 'goddam cockroach'. He was right.

Before archy was through, his work filled six volumes of poetry and any number of anthologies: *archy and mehitabel* (1927); *archy's life of mehitabel* (1933); *archy does his part* (1935); *the lives and times of archy and mehitabel* (1940); *archyology: the lost tales of archy and mehitabel* (1996); and *archyology II (the final dig)* (1998). *archy and mehitabel,* a popular 1950s musical, described as a 'back-alley opera', played successfully on Broadway. Written by Mel Brooks and Joe Darion, it starred Carol Channing, John Carradine and Edie Bracken. In 1971 it inspired John D. Winton's animated cartoon musical, *shinbone alley*.

Reprinted in Martha Paulos's delightful anthology *Insect-Asides: Great Poems on Man's Pest Friends*, and followed by one of archy's own poems, Christopher Morley's poem 'dedicated to don marquis' speaks for itself. Beginning 'Scuttle, scuttle little roach / How you run when I approach', it ends, albeit humor-ously, on a note of kinship:

Timid roach, why be so shy?
We are brothers, Thou and I.
In the midnight, like yourself,
I explore the pantry shelf.[19]

D. Keith McKevan, according to Jay Mechling the scientist responsible for some of the best historical and folk medical research on the cockroach, has written at least two poems inspired by Marquis's character: 'epitaph for archy' and 'and another for the well-known archy'. Both suggest that a deep scientific knowledge of the insect promotes the respect Marquis obviously feels for canny survivors like the cockroach.

In another vein, mystery novelist Dana Stabenow includes in *Play With Fire* a scene her detective recalls from her English 101 class at the University of Alaska.[20] The professor introduces poetry by reading first from the *Iliad* and then from *the lives and times of archy and mehitabel*. Although seemingly unrelated to the case in question, taking a 'new outlook on life', as archy is forced to when he becomes a cockroach, is key to any effective investigation of human entanglements in the Yukon as much as in the Big Apple.

Recent spin-offs have brought archy full circle. The online edition of *The San Francisco Examiner* named as its mascot a cockroach cartoon character inspired by Marquis's poet-roach. Like the East coast archy, the West coast Bernie has his own column, is addicted to apt aphorisms, and intends to serve as 'a bug in the system', a particularly apt role for a computerized cockroach! In an interview, Bernie told journalist Wayne Robins that he had accidentally sent an email to examiner.com editor Tom Parker while cavorting on some keypad. At first incredulous, Parker – like Marquis before him – succumbed to the cockroach's *vers libre*. Jim Ennes, whose web site keeps archy available to web surfers, approves.[21] Not to be undone, the East coast archy surfaced in a letter to *The New York Times* titled 'Boss, Where are the Typewriters?' to announce that mehitabel had brought him news of the rebirth of *The New York Sun*, an institution famous both for assuring Virginia that, yes, there is a Santa Claus and, of course, for its *vers libre* columnist, archy.[22]

The cockroach's use as character and urban symbol of the underside is not limited to Euro- or Latino-American works. It would require not another chapter but another book to do justice to the role of the cockroach in the urban novels and plays of the Kenyan Meja Mwangi (*The Cockroach Dance*, 1979); the South African Breyten Breytenbach (*Johnny Cockroach: A Lament for Our Times*, 1999); in the work of copper-wire sculptor Walter Oltmann and Nigerian poet Wole Soyinka ('Conversation at Night with a Cockroach', 1965). African novelists like Alex La Gama (*A Walk in the Night*) and Chinua Achebe (*The Anthills of the Savannah*, 1988) turn to the cockroach for many of the same symbolic associations, as do American writers.

Cockroaches abound in satiric and urban works by the Indonesian Norburtus Riantiarno (*Time Bomb & Cockroach Opera: Two Plays*, 1992); Egyptian Tawfig al-Hakim (*Fate of a Cockroach: Four Plays of Freedom*, 1973); Cuban Reinaldo Arenas (*The Assault*, 1990) who records a nightmarish cockroach hunt in the Concentrated Rehabilitation Camps of Castro's Cuba; Basque Bernardo Atxaga (*Obabakoak*, 1992); Londoner Richard Marsh (*The Beetle*, 1897); Canadian Alan Williams *(The Cockroach Trilogy*, 1981); and Russian Victor Pelevin (*The Life of Insects*, 1994).

On the other hand, ending such a history with this long list of virtually unexplored sources is exciting. It suggests how rich cockroach allusion and imagery is in modern literature and life, especially when the setting for the works in which it appears explores the underside of what is becoming in this day of instant communication and swift travel, a world-wide urban culture. In addition to all its other significances, the cockroach has come to represent a universal human contact and experience. It speaks a language understood by people the world over who suffer at the hands of those who sacrifice community for wealth and compassion for power.

6 Robo-roach

Recently cockroaches have become the laboratory animal of choice. Often used in school labs because they are easy to keep and breed, cockroaches are exempt from the Animal Welfare Act, lacking a legislative lobby in any country. To date their exploitation has caused few outcries from students concerned with animal welfare. Steven M. Wise, champion of legal rights for nonhuman animals, admits in *Drawing the Line* that in interviews and public talks about his first book, *Rattling the Cage*, he was challenged about where he would draw the line – 'Monkeys? Cows? Dogs? Snakes? Frogs? and (wink, wink) what about insects? Had I answered this last in the affirmative', he is sure his answer 'would have been used to counter the exceedingly powerful arguments [his book makes] for the dignity-rights of chimpanzees and bonobos.'[1] Yet, after the studies that form the basis of *Drawing the Line*, what he learned about honeybees makes him reconsider the question of insect rights.

Had he studied the cockroach, he would have found himself in a similar quandary. ABC News Online reported that at a recent symposium held by the Universities Federation on Animal Welfare, Dr Stephen Wick argued that 'If a chimp pulls its hand away after an electric shock, we say she presumably must have felt the analogous subjective experience . . .

we call pain, but cockroaches, slugs, and snails – which are not protected by legislation – also react the same way.'

Cockroaches, prone to cancerous tumours like the ones humans get, have been useful in cancer research at least since 1913 when Danish pathologist Johannes Fibiger induced cancerous tumours in mice and rats by feeding them cockroaches infected with *Spiroptera*, demonstrating for the first time that cancer can be caused by external stimulus (carcinogens).

Richard Karp, an immunologist at the University of Cincinnati, recently disproved the assumption that invertebrates lack true immune responses. In the long-living cockroach, he discovered not only an immune system but a sophisticated one with similarities to the human immune system. Thus, as in humans, female cockroaches have stronger immune responses than males and the very young and very old have weaker responses than mature adults.[2]

Berta Scharrer, State University of New York at Old Westbury, Long Island, one of the world's leading authorities on the cockroach, 'diced up and delved into cockroach brains for insights into the [human] nervous system'. Like our own cells, the cockroach's nerve cells secrete hormones into the blood, effectively allowing the brain (cockroach or human) to communicate with the body. Her first specimens, *Leucophaea mederae*, arrived unsought in a shipment of lab monkeys from South America in the 1940s. Nearly 5 cm (2 inches) long, this handsome walnut cockroach clicks loudly when it moves, has a distinctive musky odour, and flies.

After Scharrer's death in 1995 six aluminum pens containing hundreds of her roaches were left to her research students and assistants and the descendants of these roaches continue to provide insights – to their detriment and our benefit – about the workings of the brain and nervous system. Whole new areas of specialization like neuro-endocrinology and psycho-endocrinology developed because of Scharrer's work. Interestingly, much of what the cockroaches revealed 'helped guide Western scientists toward a modern empirical understanding of the ancient mind-body precepts of Eastern medicine', work for which Scharrer received a Nobel Prize nomination in 1983.[3]

Still more has been learned in the genetic experiments of Mary Ross, founder of the Genetic Stock Center for the German Cockroach at Virginia Polytechnic Institute. She has produced between 40 and 50 mutant cockroach strains over the past 30 years, one of them a pale purple-eyed beauty. Another carries a sterility factor, which may prove useful in meeting the goals of the laboratory's underwriter. Much like Jennyanydots, the Gumbie Cat in T. S. Eliot's *Old Possum's Book of Practical Cats*, Ross is convinced she can solve her household's vermin problem with a little remedial breeding (Jennyanydots turned her cockroaches into a scout troop). Cockroaches have also played basic roles in studies of animal behaviour, of the human nervous system, as well as of human nutrition, movement and metabolism.

As a result of such research, whether in the name of social reform or extermination, much has been learned about cockroach intelligence, evasiveness, endurance, speed, sex and breeding habits – not the least of which is how closely they resemble humans. But little of that knowledge seems to have convinced researchers of Stephen Wick's point that cockroaches react to pain as does any sentient creature. Cockroaches are still enduring pain without reward or sympathy or legal protection for the benefit of non-cockroaches like ourselves.

That human failure to identify with the cockroach persists despite its scientific use as a substitute for human systems was recently made clear. University of Michigan experimenters attached wires to the backs of live cockroaches, sending an electrical current through their legs and antennae to make them move. In Japan, Tsukuba University's team, selecting American cockroaches as their subjects – presumably because they are the hardest of all the cockroaches to kill, gassed them with carbon dioxide before removing their wings and antennae to replace them with electrodes which force them to turn and go forward or backward. In April 1997, the E-zine *boot* reported that a University spokesperson explained that 'electronically enhanced insects . . . could be used effectively for search and rescue missions or even espionage surveillance'. And PETA's Holiday 1996 issue reported that when queried, University of Michigan experimenters said 'Biobots' could be used to carry small packages of screws.

The advent of Robo-roaches, live cockroaches implanted with remote-control devices, received virtually no coverage in the popular press. But when researchers announced in May 2002 that rats had had their brains wired with tiny electrodes and could be controlled by remotes, *The New York Times* and *The Boston Globe* editorial pages both carried pieces on the event the following Sunday. Both emphasized exactly the same thing: as goes the rat, so could we humans go! The shorter piece in the *Times* 'Week in Review' compares the pleasurable impulses that lead the rat to follow directions with our own reaction should we follow directions and be rewarded with the taste of 'luxurious dark chocolate'. The longer *Globe* editorial finds the news 'darn scary' because these animal trials are recognized as 'nascent experiments in mind control'. The question is why the heightened reaction to robo-rats when no similar panic resulted from robo-roaches? Apparently, despite the scientific evidence, the assumption is that rats, being mammals, have minds like ours. Cockroaches, being insects, don't.

Numbers, the cockroach narrator of Daniel Weiss's novel *The Roaches Have No King* admits, 'Humans don't think much of the intelligence of insects,' but goes on to show just how inadequate that judgment is. The amazing thing to Numbers is that humans continue to spread boric acid powder, assuming the cockroaches will cooperatively stroll through it despite its 'astringent taste and all [the cockroach's] knowledge of its effects'.[4] Apparently the writer of a 1972 article in *Science Digest* predicting boric acid as 'the ultimate weapon,' had forgotten when he called his piece 'ARCHY on the Run: New War with an Old Weapon', that cockroach poets can both read and write. Within months it was clear the 'ultimate weapon' had been defused by cockroach genes and intelligence, neither of which had been figured into the mix.

Weiss's cockroach narrator finds it equally amazing that humans spend a fortune on Roach Motels, strategically placing them to attract their quarry when 'one viewing of *Psycho* on TV had kept us away from it. And in case anyone had missed the show, the box described its adhesive, even the recipe of its cloying bait, right on the side. Only an illiterate with a taste for Kandy Korn would ever walk into a Roach Motel.'[5]

The anonymous human author of *The Autobiography of Alexander Fever* has his cockroach narrator explain that, through an evolutionary advancement some 2 million years ago, all cockroaches are born with the sum of all cockroach knowledge logged in their DNA – 'a simple technique of micro-engineering accomplished within the ootheca itself'. In sum, each individual remembers 'the entire history of this planet since the Great Age of the Cockroach some 350 million years ago'. Thus the life-story of each individual cockroach 'encapsulates . . . the entire history of the species'. Even if one doubts that real cockroaches share these fictional roaches' ability to read, despite their centuries of consuming the written word, Numbers and Alexander have a point or two in cockroaches' favour here.[6]

The intelligence of the cockroach has been studied at least since 1912 when African-American C. H. Turner at Summer Teacher's College in St Louis conducted behavioural research that proved the cockroach was far smarter than humans had assumed. Not only could they learn even to overcome their innate aversion to light, but they proved to be one of the few animals smart enough to learn to run a maze. In fact, once learned by painful electric shock, they would proceed to run the maze even headless because, unlike humans, cockroach brains are distributed throughout their bodies. Beheading will kill them because, of course, they cannot eat, but it will not rob them of their memory, a fact I am sure cockroaches find comforting.

Other cockroach research has received more attention. Wood cockroaches' (*Cryptocercus*) microbial symbionts, first discovered and filmed in the 1930s by Harvard entomologist Lemuel Roscoe Cleveland, continued to fascinate and inform the scientist until his death in 1969. Cleveland was struck by the size of the symbionts – 'some nearly half a millimeter in length – 10 times their typical size', by their harbouring of 'smaller protists and bacteria', and by the protists' habit of consuming one another. As Margulis and Sagan put it:

In the swollen rear intestine of these large Virginia roaches he discovered a sealed world of protists living with almost no oxygen. Swimming inside were corkscrew-shaped bacteria called spirochetes. Still-tinier rod bacteria dwelled and reproduced in even larger numbers. And . . . among this entourage were 'giant' cells almost half-a-millimeter in length, looming over the smaller creatures like an aircraft or giant submarine. [7]

Cleveland guessed that their cannibalism and partial digestion with the resulting partial merging of predator and prey served both to feed and to allow them to reproduce and evolve. His paper on the origins of sexual reproduction was published in *Science* in 1949 but sparked no interest until Lynn Margulis, now a professor in the Department of Geosciences at the University of Massachusetts at Amherst, followed its lead to the revolutionary theory that such symbiosis accounts both for the origin of the cell and of sexual fertilization. It is fitting, I think, that a creature as ancient as *Cryptocercus* – and the even older world duplicated by conditions in their guts – should reveal to us that our method of reproduction is, in effect, a bacteria's improvement on one billion-year-old protist cannibalism.

Modern electron microscopes have allowed researchers to peer ever more closely into the cockroach's inner life, often without harming them. Electron microscopes use a beam of electrons for their light source and have electromagnetic lenses that control and focus the beams. The micrographs are high resolution black and white images that clearly show details about the insect's anatomy never revealed before. Human research on the cockroach has often been far more invasive than Cleveland's, than electro-magnetic imaging or even Turner's beheading of some of his maze-trained specimens.

The cockroach was a subject of choice both when safe radiation doses were being established and again when the Space Program was establishing safe limits of gravity for astronauts. It was found that a human astronaut would pass out at 12 Gs – 12 times the force of Earth's gravity – and his internal organs collapse at 18 Gs. The cockroach, however, was still conscious and

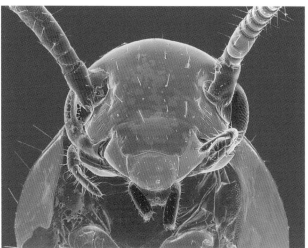

'Bug Band' by Tina Carvalho, using images taken through electron microscopes.

The cockroach drummer.

skittering around happily at 126 GS. That has led to plans for using cockroaches and a few other insects (milkweed bugs, dragonfly nymphs and ants) to transform the environment of Mars, perhaps even in time to make it habitable for man.

Whereas a human will die when exposed to 600 rads of radiation, cockroaches have been shown to survive 830, dying only when doses reach around 3,200 rads. In research on the American cockroach (*Periplaneta americana*) in 1959 it was found that half of a colony exposed to 10,000 rads was still alive 2 weeks after exposure – long enough for egg-cases to be laid and hatched, ensuring the survival of the species after the parents succumbed.

Zapping insects with radiation – not to mention the numerous poisons developed to kill them – has piqued the imaginations of numerous writers of science fiction and horror novels and films resulting in a swarm of 1940s and '50s B-movie monster bugs, beginning with the atomically spawned giant ants of *Them!* (1954). Actually film makers have exploited our fear of insects at least since 1896 when a short subject, *Une nuit terrible*, was released by French film innovator Georges Méliès, but it was the greater fear produced by the splitting of the atom that gave insect films and insects as subjects of scientific experimentation a terrifying thematic thrust. Acting a little like cicadas, these films seem to have gone underground to hatch and swarm again in the 1970s and again in the 1990s; the way things are going, they are probably gearing up for another infestation not far in the future.

The 1970s produced two cockroach films that take the role of the cockroach as experimental animal seriously. Although the pyrotechnic cockroaches in the now classic film *Bug* (1975) – based on a good novel, *The Hephaestus Plague* (1973), by Thomas Page – emerge from the depths of Earth when an earthquake of major proportion rocks the California coast, it is the obsession of entomologist James Parmiter that rescues them from a natural demise in the unsupportive surface environment in which they find themselves. By breeding them with healthy surface cockroaches, Parmiter produces a species of 25 cm (10 inch) super-intelligent, potentially deadly creatures who belch fire, eat raw meat and are impervious to known insecticides.

In a twist not common to films or novels in this genre, the insects are also intelligent, using their bodies to spell out messages to their creator with the cooperative intelligence of true social insects. Rather than an 'evil . . . from the bowels of the earth', as Jay Mechling sees them,[8] they are survivors who, finding themselves in an alien environment, want only to return to their home at the centre of the earth. Ultimately they do so, taking their creator with them in a particularly violent but perfectly just sequence since it is the scientist, not the cockroaches, whose uncontrolled meddling with nature has created the evil in Riverside.

The Nest, released in 1988, is more typical of the apocalyptic trend that began in films in the United States in the 1950s but took a new turn after news of the first successful genetic transformation of an insect was published in 1983.[9] Based on the novel *The Nest* (1980) by Gregory A. Douglas – a pen name of Eli Cantor – the film posits that a failed genetic engineering experiment intended to control resident cockroaches results in the creation of large, hungry cockroaches whose taste soon turns from the pest cockroaches they were bred to gobble-up to larger prey when they escape on an island off Cape Cod, Massachusetts. After eating the glue off the books in the town library, they turn to the island's domestic animals and marginal humans. Apparently the genetic tinkering also changed the cockroaches' breeding habits, making them social insects like

Roaches have never tasted flesh... until now.

She's just an appetizer.

MGM/UA HOME VIDEO

THE NEST

IT WAS AN ORDINARY CAPE COD TOWN – UNTIL THE HUGE MUTANTS BEGAN TO LEAVE THEIR NEST.
BY GREGORY A. DOUGLAS

The novel and video covers both suggest that *The Nest* is a classic horror story, but the film's is the more sensational.

the closely related termite and, worse, they are also beginning to mutate into whatever they consume – the source of some really gross scenes that audiences love and which inspired the 2001 film *Mimic*. At any rate when a female entomologist from INTEC arrives at North Port, she finally locates the nest of the cockroach queen and, showing equal determination for the survival of her human kind, manages to detonate a bomb that seals the nest off, thus saving the island and what humans remain on it.

Experimental roaches play leading roles in the February 1996 *X-Files* episode 'The War of the Coprophages' (dung-eaters) written by Morgan Darin. It boasts a Stephen Hawking-like robotics genius who develops bionic robo-roaches not unlike those being developed in universities in both the United States and Japan. 'War of the Coprophages' is set in Miller's Grove, Massachusetts, perhaps because of a real-life 'Attack of the Mutant Madagascar Cockroaches' that took place in Natick, Massachusetts in 1974. The US Army Natick Laboratory had carried out secret experiments on the effects of radiation on a host of Madagascar hissing roaches, disposing of them by bagging them in plastic garbage bags, throwing in some carbon tetrachloride, and hiring a local dump company to haul them off to the Natick and Randolf town dumps. Someone must have forgotten that carbon tetrachloride melts plastic but has no ill effects on the cases of cockroach oothecae. Soon neighbouring homeowners were reporting infestations of what they called 'turtle bugs', a euphemism that did not keep their neighbourhood from being dubbed 'Cockroach Corners' – or do much for resale values.

Although the local Boards of Health assured the public that the cockroaches were not a health threat, it is not surprising that locals found it disconcerting to find 10 cm (4 inch) cockroaches pouring out of their breakfast cereal boxes. The towns sprayed the areas with chlordane and the Army, which had originally denied its involvement, finally provided DDT, by then illegal, a combination that ended the 'plague' in the spring of 1975, nine months after it had begun. (One wonders if the New England winter wouldn't have accomplished as much unaided.) The incident would have gone unnoticed had not *The Boston Globe*'s exposé of toxic sites and contaminated ground water in Natick, the result of the laboratory and the cleanup of the cockroach spill, finally made it public.[10]

While there are no alien cockroaches other than those in Mulder's imagination in the *X-Files* episode, there are real cockroaches – a whole house of them under the care of entomologist

Bambi ('Her name is Bambi?') Berenbaum, a pun on the real-life, much published entomologist May Berenbaum who, in addition to writing bug-friendly books, sponsors the Insect Fear Festival at the University of Illinois at Urbana-Champaign. (Berenbaum, incidentally, lists, as the number one fear factor in insect horror movies, our fear that science will go awry.) The *X-Files'* Berenbaum character also loves insects, especially cockroaches. She explains to Mulder, who cannot understand what 'a girl like you' is doing in a house infested with cockroaches, that she loves them because of their 'beauty and honesty'. 'Honesty?' the smitten but confused Mulder asks. 'Eat, sleep, defecate, procreate,' the lovely Bambi replies. 'That's all they do and all they pretend to do. Of course, that's all that humans do too, but they try to make more of it.'

Her suggestion that cockroaches may eat dung but that they aren't full of bullshit like humans silences Mulder, who, like reviewer Sarah Stegall, 'loved the idea of a war between native Earth cockroaches and invaders in the guise of Blattaria (cockroaches), a fight carried on under our noses (or in them) without our being aware of it'. Although that war does not materialize in the episode, there is a central scene in which Mulder, still not convinced some of the roaches are not alien invaders, stares into a cockroach's eyes and murmurs 'Welcome to planet Earth!' And for just a minute he – and the audience – see through the cockroach's multiple vision, a scene echoing one of the most famous of all insect-science gone awry films, *The Fly* (1958).

Other robo-roaches provide work for special effects artists in films like *Damnation Alley* (1977); *Men in Black* (1997); *Mimic* (1997); *The Fifth Element* (1977) in which a bio-roach with a microphone implant makes a cameo appearance; *LEXX*, in which a trio of human misfits travel a parallel universe in a giant bioengineered insect; and *Starship Troopers* (1997). Based on Roger Zelansky's 1969 novel of the same name, *Damnation Alley* loses the thematic force of the novel and produces giant flesh-eating cockroaches that are jokes compared to the insects produced by the special effects of later films. In *The World of Fantasy Films*, Richard Meyers writes that it is 'obvious that most of the creatures are models pasted on rugs which are pulled across the floor with ropes.'[11] It's hard to take the film seriously, although the novel is one of what science fiction great Thomas Disch called the 'postnuclear playgrounds' of its time, complete with 'mutated, carnivorous high-camp cockroaches.'[12]

Men in Black (1997), original screenplay by Ed Solomon (later novelized by Steve Perry), is a comedy based on a comic book series by Lowell Cunningham. The series proposes that millions of out-of-work extraterrestrials have sought harbour on Earth, blending in peacefully and unnoticed by all but a top-secret agency concerned with terrestrial safety – Mr Jones and Mr Smith, the Men in Black. Their assignment is to license and monitor the aliens and protect earthlings from any bad seeds that may turn up – the worst of whom, predictably, is Edgar who looks and acts like a cockroach. Hated and feared by humans and extraterrestrials alike, he actually doesn't even look much like a cockroach, but the association is confirmed by 'the real cockroaches that drop out of its sleeve throughout the movie'.[13]

Inspired certainly by *Alien* (1979) and perhaps by the cockroaches so large men had to fight them with shotguns in H. G. Wells's *The Food of the Gods* (1904), a short story by Donald Wolheim provided the plot and theme for Guillermo Del Toro's *Mimic* (1997). *Mimic*'s entomologists develop a mutant strain of huge hybrids to kill the existing cockroaches responsible for spreading a deadly virus among the city's humans. The mutant insects are genetically programmed to die after six months of killing virus-laden fellow-bugs. Clearly genetic manipulation is the newer version of the radiation dangers warned of in the earlier film, *The Nest*.

We all know what happens next! Instead of dying, the mutants begin to replicate, grow larger, and soon acquire the ability to mimic their human predators, breaking more boundaries. Actually a cross between termite and praying mantis, they look too much like the cockroach, a close relative of both, for viewers to assume they are anything else. In fact *Newsweek*'s Ray Sawhill called *Mimic* 'the best mutant-cockroach horror thriller ever made' and comments on its relationship to earlier cult classics from Italian vampire movies of the 1960s (he should also have mentioned director Del Toro's 1992 Mexican creepy vampire film *Cronos*) and to 1985's *Re-Animator* before dismissing it as 'an exploitation movie with artistic touches', but one that increases our fear 'about all the creatures we share our cities with'. Here, as in *The Nest*, a female scientist – eager herself to procreate – tackles and outwits the fertile Queen of the mutant creatures.[14]

Of course robotic cockroaches also flourish in literature, some of which influenced the film depictions. Following on from William S. Burroughs, whose cockroach character is a robot-like typewriter-cockroach, and the science fiction of Philip K. Dick, infestations of robotic cockroaches threaten the earth in Lance Olson's short story 'Kamikaze Motives of the Immaculate Deconstruction in the Data-Sucking Rust-Age of Insectile Hackers'. Olson, one of the foremost proponents of a literary movement called Avant-Pop, while highly experimental in method, finds the cockroach as useful a vehicle for social satire as have many mainstream authors, and there is something appealing in the story's premise that 'all of the disturbing media events of the last twenty years have been engineered by an infestation of robotic cockroaches who are turning Earth into a sordid reality-entertainment channel for the amusement of the rest of the galaxy'.[15]

The fad has reached even into the realm of children's literature. In P. J. Neri's Hawaii Chillers series is a 1998 volume called *Killer Cockroaches* in which the father of young heroes Drew and Corey is kidnapped by giant mutant cockroaches. The plot sets them about zapping these villains before the cockroaches grow even larger and eat them and their father alive. In comparison with these monsters spawned by radiation or genetic experimentation, actual bionic and non-bionic robo-roaches are pretty benign, more like Franky, the 'monster' bug created from the parts of giant insects in Steven Cousins's *Frankenbug*, who is only one-part predator and many-parts browser and scavenger. Somehow a monster who prefers marshmallows to flesh falls short of terror.

Roboticist Martin Buehler's equally benign Rttex O is a walking robot based on cockroach anatomy. Australian roboticist Rodney Brooks, founder of the Insect Lab at the Massachusetts Institute of Technology, is developing cockroach-like bots, while at Case Western Reserve, Randy Beer's Robot III is remarkably like a real cockroach except it is 75 cm (30 in) long and weighs 14 kilos (31 lbs). Ultimately, they claim, it will do practical, useful things. News that an entomologist at the University of Illinois has built robot cockroaches 45 cm (18 in) long and plans one at least 120 cm long led columnist Dave Barry to ask, 'Why do we need to create giant cockroaches?'[16] The fact is that now robo-roaches have become successful techno-toys, they have proved themselves good for the economy.

The brightly coloured plastic b.i.o. Bugs (Bio-Mechanical Integrated Organisms) based on NASA technology from

Hasbro's Wow Wee Toys division hit the toy market in 2001. For $29.95, ten dollars less than B.I.O. Bugs, you can purchase the Ultimate Robot Kit from Dorling Kindersley and construct and programme your own CreepycrawlyBot. Energized by an AA battery, this cardboard model will lumber over obstacles on its six legs as ably as do the really expensive versions produced by MIT artificial intelligence and robotics experts.[17] Michael B. Binnard's project Boadicea produced a small six-legged walking robot built of lightweight materials.

When robot Boadicea runs, all its legs provide vertical force to propel it forward. But the front legs also provide brakes and are able to reach up or down on uneven terrain while the rear legs are powerfully propulsive. The middle legs are versatile, able to serve either to propel or brake. They can stand-in for front or rear limbs should those be damaged and can pitch the body up to climb over an obstacle while the rear legs provide the push that vaults the insect over whatever is in its way.[18]

In December 1999, *The New York Times Magazine* reported that Jason Lanier and his colleagues were developing literate bio-roaches by translating literary works from computer code to 4-digit DNA language and splicing the information onto apparently functionless strands of the cockroaches' DNA. The archiving is reinforced with an interbreeding program, which will 'ensure the genetic transmission' of the information. If successful, soon every roach in New York City will be a scuttling repository of western culture (although whether humans will be able to access it remains a question). At the very least Lanier's plan would enable humans and roaches, at least theoretically according to their creators, to 'coexist in a new [cultural] symbiotic relationship' based on shared culture as well as on the evolutionary history we now share. Perhaps Lanier means that if we colonized the roach as we have

Boadicea, an early six-legged, pneumatically powered walking robot designed at the Massachusetts Institute of Technology.

colonized so many humans we've judged to be other, we could acknowledge our kinship to the roach and to the rest of the planet's fauna without the fear that now makes us hate and exploit them.

7 The Golden Cockroach

> At our feet, in the center of this sacred circle, is a shimmering
> golden roach. This is a good omen for the future.
>
> Marcia Luack, *At the Pool of Wonder*, (1989)

Famed entomologist Edward O. Wilson in his most recent
book, *The Future of Life*, addresses the spirit of Henry Thoreau:
the wilderness of yesterday, with its wolves and pumas may
have vanished, in fact did not exist in Thoreau's day, but the
micro-wilderness that existed under Thoreau's feet supports
the feet of visitors to Walden Pond, Concord, Massachusetts,
today. In the leaf litter and the soil beneath it flourish tens of
thousands of diverse creatures, many stranger than 'the things
you see in Star Wars'. On a recent visit to Walden Pond, Wilson
pointed out under one log, 'a predatory rove beetle, a millipede,
a spiderling, a nematode . . . ants and a wood cockroach'. He
immediately began to describe to *New York Times* reporter
James Gorman, who accompanied Wilson here as part of an
interview, 'the thousands of inoffensive species of cockroach
throughout the world' living in 'a world as wild as it was before
humans came to . . . North America'.[1]

Despite recent high tech capabilities and acquired urban
associations, the cockroach continues to prefer life in such
untrammelled wildernesses worldwide. The vast majority of
cockroach species still live under woodpiles or in the leaf-litter
of forests, or under the bark of trees where their scavenging con-
tributes to the creative compost on which all life depends for
growth and renewal. Perhaps because they impose less on what

humans grasp most tenaciously as human territory, wild cock-roaches are, when they are given any human attention, more accurately chronicled by humans than are their city cousins. Researchers and artists alike, beginning with Maria Sibylla Merian in the early eighteenth century and, I hope, not ending with Wilson in the twenty-first, see wild cockroaches as fasci-natingly beautiful, diverse and successful life forms uniquely adapted to planet Earth. The All-Species Inventory promises by the year 2026 to identify an estimated 7–100 million species of earth-dwellers, yet undiscovered cockroaches among them.[2]

It is more than coincidence that the best essay on Merian's life and work in English appears in *Women on the Margins: Three Seventeenth Century Lives* (1995) by Natalie Zemon Davis. Refusing to be confined to the margins as women and women artists and naturalists of her time were, Merian had a special affinity for creatures like the cockroach, also condemned to the margins. She uses her study of the metamorphosis of the Surinam albino cockroach as the frontispiece for a second edition (1719) of her *Metamorphosis Insectorum Surinamensium*. For Davis the most striking thing about this plate is how it embraces Merian's theme and narrative, a theme and narra-tive technique learned from her work by John James Audubon. Perhaps she even exceeds Audubon in making her theme – metamorphosis – speak for what would be recognized today as ecofeminist concerns.

Researchers and travellers concerned to look beyond the obvious fact that many tropical cockroaches are brightly coloured, find amazing creatures. When Carolyn Alexander decided to follow in the footprints of Mary Kingsley, another fearless nineteenth-century traveller, in the 1980s, she provides a far more appreciative glimpse of the cockroach in the grot-toes of Latoursville in Gabon, Africa, than are suggested by

Kingsley's own encounters. Kingsley, apparently terrified of caves, went no further than the portals, but Alexander enters: 'In the swinging light of the lantern, I could see that the rocks on either side were encrusted with crabs and guarded by unyielding cockroaches with foot-long feelers' thriving on bat guano.[3] They strike Alexander as sentinels ushering her in to a Journey to the

This drawing by Joe Bullock is based on an unusually shaped Tropical Cockroach belonging to the family Blattellidae.

Underworld from which the traveller emerges 'possessed of new knowledge, direction, and a sense of one's destiny', an appreciative response to the chthonic associations of the cockroach also very in tune with the ecofeminist vision.

Similarly, the space-traveller in Kilgore Trout's (Kurt Vonnegut's) novel *Venus on the Half-Shell* (1974) found, at the end of his odyssey, a large cockroach whose knowledge changes his view of the universe. Vonnegut's Bingo is 'a hoary old cock-roachoid' as old as creation itself who tells Simon that his universe and all the others that exist are scientific experiments and that when a people kills off their own planet – as they seem invariably to do, his kind (the Hoonhors), whose home planet is a trillion miles away from earth, spring into action, cleaning up the mess by salting the atmosphere so that heavy rains wash away the debris. That Simon begins his journey on Ararat suggests, of course, that this is not the first time Earth has been saved from human error. When Simon asks Bingo why It (the Creator) persists, when It must realize the agony experienced by living beings on the planets that fail, Bingo cuts off his question with a belch and a counter question with which the novel ends: 'Why not?'[4] The Creator, at least the legendary version, is no ecofeminist, but fortunately the Hoonhors are!

In the nonfiction world of Peru, Australia and Madagascar, all once a part of Gondwanaland, giant cockroaches almost the size of Trout's do exist, but such tropical habitats also harbour exquisite red, yellow and blue species. Perhaps the first to describe such a tropical beauty in fiction was the English writer Christopher Blayre. In a 1921 short story he describes a stunning blue cockroach imported with a bunch of bananas:

> It was a most lovely beast. In shape and size identical with the cockroaches which stay among one's brushes on board ship, and architecturally indistinguishable from the larger members of the Kitchen family, the Blue Cockroach was clad in a pure, pale azure, as if a cunning artificer in enamels had fashioned it, and had given to its surface a texture of the finest smooth velvet. Its long antennae waved inquiringly back and forth, its tiny eyes

sparkled black with crimson points, and then it began to run. The professor caught it . . . as it toppled from the edge of the counter. It bit him.[5]

The significant point in the story is less that such beautiful cockroaches exist, than that its bite delivers an 'infection' that stimulates the Professor's passions, particularly his sexual drive, almost overcoming the reticence that has kept him without wife or children. For Blayre the Blue Cockroach, like Luack's Golden Cockroach, is a conduit to the primal, to fertility as well as emotional and instinctual honesty.

A living golden cockroach, the Little Yellow Cockroach (*Cariblatta lutea*), is a dainty creature barely a quarter of an inch long, named for its clear yellowish to light brown colour, with a distinguishing pattern of black marks on its pronotum. It lives, virtually invisibly, in the leaf-litter of dry forests from the West Indies to the southeastern United States, as far north as Raleigh and Roanoke Island, North Carolina.[6] Larger cousins, such as those remembered by the Chicano immigrants in Anna Castillo's short story 'Christmas Story of the Golden Cockroach', do dwell in tropical rainforests. Their ancestors, distant and not so distant, associated golden roaches with the sacred maize that symbolizes growth and procreation. For them a golden roach is one of the elemental powers, not unlike D. H. Lawrence's 'The Snake', equally associated with darkness and light, death and life – the natural cycle. Luack suggests that

the pairing of gold, that enduring essence that symbolizes the soul, with the ancient insect that has both preceded and accompanied us in our evolutionary journey signifies that some great work is underway – a deep recognition and healing called forth from the primordial wisdom that is held in the heart of creation.[7]

Possibly that explains why the cockroach has become a feminist and now an ecofeminist icon in the work of poets like Muriel Rukeyser, Anne Sexton, Maxine Kumin, Vivian Shipley, Caroline Frazer and Linda Hogan and of fiction writers like Clarice Lispector, Jane Smiley and Penny Perkins. Its positive presentation in the work of contemporary children's writers should also be seen in this light, reminding us, as the ecofeminist canon does, that children, like women and other 'minorities', have been marginalized by the patriarchy.

Mary Pope Osborne prefaces her children's novel *Spider Kane and the Mystery Under the May-Apple* (1999) with lines from Christina Rossetti that express the theme of all these works:

The last and least of things
That soar on quivering wings,
Or crawl among the grass blades out of sight
Have just as clear a right
To their appointed portion of delight
As queens or kings.

Janelle Cannon's *Crickwing* depicts a beautiful though damaged golden rainforest roach who becomes the culture hero of his leaf-cutter ant neighbours by outwitting invader army ants – with his leaf sculptures. However fanciful the author/artist's treatment of her nonhuman characters, each brightly coloured book contains notes on the actual biology and evolutionary history of its protagonist and, in the case of *Crickwing*, of leaf-cutter ants as well as of cockroaches. The cockroach notes make clear that Cannon's intentions are to counter the bad reputation of

Crickwing appeared in 2000. The author and illustrator Janelle Cannon is known as a champion of the under-appreciated.

the cockroach by emphasizing how few of their myriad species interfere with human business.

Crickwing, a wild green-gold cockroach, she tells her young readers, lives only in the rainforest. Another wild roach 'spends much of its life diving in ponds and rivers, eating decayed leaves, dead fish, and algae'. One of the rarest tropical roaches, 'the Tuna Cave Cockroach in Puerto Rico . . . may soon be added to the endangered species list'. And Cannon's notes conclude, 'Considering how long these well-designed bugs have survived . . . it is easy to see that we humans invaded the cockroaches' pantry long before the cockroach entered ours!'

Mystery in Bugtown (1998) acknowledges that its cockroach character, Charlie Roach, is both an outcast and a victim.

Most if not all of the cockroach characters in children's literature belong to the domestic species and live in familiar urban settings. Cannon's notes tell us that she sees domestic species as involuntary immigrants who, finding themselves in unfamiliar and often hostile environments, survived by taking advantage of human dwellings 'full of warmth and food that help cockroaches thrive'. Clearly in Cannon's mind, wild and domestic cockroaches alike are variously threatened and have species-specific gifts to enrich the community. They are seen as individuals with stories to tell who are worthy of our interest and concern.

Children are an unbiased audience for cockroach narratives and for cockroach encounters. Commenting on the engaging enthusiasm of the 73-year-old E. O. Wilson for his 'field trip' discoveries at Walden Pond, reporter James Gorman commented that the entomologist's 'sense of purpose and pleasure . . . would instantly make any 10-year-old join him'. This is the sense of wonder Rachel Carson alludes to and what, in *Biophilia*, Wilson himself refers to as 'a formula of reenchantment' capable of penetrating into the 'untrammeled wild'.[8]

Researchers have recently found that, up to the age of four, children show no aversion to roaches although soon thereafter many refuse to drink from a glass containing a plastic model cockroach. Unfortunately, their prejudice against cockroaches is only one of many absorbed at this tender age from the cultures in which they live. Without such myopia, the cockroach, instead of inspiring disgust, can reawaken the indigenous, earth-centeredness it once symbolized in cultures threatened by European colonial invaders.

Philippine artist Manuel Ocampo, now working in California, has produced a number of large canvases in which images of cockroaches are surrounded by symbols of Spanish colonization and the Catholic conversion of his native island.[9] The Maltese novelist Francis Ebejer also uses the cockroach for this purpose in *Evil of the Cockroach King* (1960). Like the cockroaches native to the island, Ebejer's characters must dig themselves 'into the soil, amid rock, scrub and mysterious caverns in the cliffsides', reasserting that long before colonialism they had 'sprung from' the island's roots. Until they achieve this, the cockroach will seem, rather than indigenous totem, an evil menace.[10]

As the twentieth century drew to a close, novelist Penny Perkins's *Bob Bridges: An Apocalyptic Fable* predicted, as does Marc Estrin's later novel *Insect Dreams*, the end of the world as humans know it, though not the end of Earth or of the cockroach. The novel embraces the by now clichéd assumption that the cockroach will survive us, that it is able to absorb radiation that would finish us, as well as deplete most of the life-supports we depend on. However, in keeping with its ecofeminist roots, the novel assures us that, once rid of man, life itself begins anew.

Bob Bridges, the novel's human protagonist, has a dream that even he recognizes as a post-Cold War era B horror movie: huge mutant insects spawned by nuclear radiation carry him off to Bugville, the Earth – or what's left of it – of the future. When Bob actually gets to the world that remains after global nuclear explosions 'set off a chain reaction of natural catastrophes' unlike any in the previous eons of the planet's history, he finds the bugs of his dreams, their increased size having been necessary for them to accomplish the work they are now destined to do.

By the time Bob arrives in their time, the cockroaches have evolved to actually metabolize the planet's still radioactive atmosphere. 'Radio-synthesis', Cock explains, is the 'third incarnation of photosynthesis'. The first, like all of 'life's essential biotechnologies', had been invented by bacteria 3.5 billion years ago. The second, possible as blue-green algae evolved, combined hydrogen with carbon dioxide, the waste product of which, oxygen, paved the road for oxygen-breathing life forms a billion years later. Now, in the third rebalancing, the roaches, viruses and bacteria were metabolizing radiation: 'as a waste

from 99 Uses for a dead cockroach

product, instead of producing green-house gases . . . [they were] excreting fumes comprised primarily of ozone' – ozone which over the years was healing the rupture that prevented the planet's receiving only filtered rays from the sun.[11]

David Quammen, whose 'A Republic of Cockroaches: When the Ultimate Exterminator Meets the Ultimate Pest' appeared in *Outside* magazine in May 1983, was inspired to write the essay by reading Jonathan Schell's *The Fate of the Earth*, a non-fiction work that makes essentially the same apocalyptic prophecy Perkins makes in *Bob Bridges*. In his chapter 'A Republic of Insects and Grasses', Schell writes convincingly of the likelihood of a nuclear Armageddon in which high levels of radiation kill all but plants and phytophagous species like crickets, mantids, walking sticks and cockroaches.

What Quammen and Schell saw as tragedy (the extinction of the human species), poet Caroline Frazer – like Perkins – sees as restoration of a natural order that, in time, would benefit the planet if not the humans who are responsible for the problem. Frazer, having given up on humans (or at least on what ecofeminists would call the patriarchal order), recommends turning 'the government /over to the insects, for the tidy digestion /of all that dung . . . / Let it be done.'[12] Cockroaches remained in touch with 'the rhythms of nature', whereas man had lost touch, not only with external but also with his 'internal rhythms', making the human species useless as a candidate for reclaiming the earth.[13]

Such warnings should enable the current power structure to recognize the danger of proceeding on our present course, of relying on traditional patriarchal culture stories. The need for a healing, life-supporting culture story seems clear. Perhaps because she looks at insects with the eyes of her American Indian progenitors, poet Linda Hogan sees the possibility of humans ceasing their war with the nature by surrendering to 'the arcane [the mysterious knowledge] of insects', to the magic 'gold powder that lets wings fly', to the 'singing/made of light and dust'. In 'Small Life' she recommends embracing the roach because 'Its shining back/and hair thin feet' create a significant part of the 'night's music', music that brings us the most important message of all, the message that 'we are safe/we are never alone'.[14]

The emergence of the cockroach as an ecofeminist icon, as unlikely a role as that may seem for such a traditionally demonized creature, was predicted in the early 1970s by poets Muriel Rukeyser and Anne Sexton and even earlier by the Brazilian novelist Clarice Lispector who is credited with bringing a woman's sensibility to the existential novel. In Lispector's *The Passion According to G. H.* (1964), the female protagonist's encounter with a cockroach in her maid's room leads her to a new acceptance of her natural rather than merely her social self – 'at the level of the cockroach . . . the most primary divine life'.

Sexton's 'Cockroach', a segment of her *Bestiary U.S.A.*, first published in *45 Mercy Street* (1974), also revalues the roach. Although it appears at the opening of the poem bearing the title 'foulest of creatures', the poet works a metamorphosis. By the end of the poem, anticipating what becomes a common metamorphosis in the later twentieth century, we share instead of this hatred, the instinct of one of Sexton's former students who, seeing her teacher threaten to stomp on a cockroach, 'picked it

That IMAX chose the cockroach to usher its young female viewer into its enchanted kingdom is in itself comment on the changing image of the cockroach in the 21st century.

161

up/in her hands and held it from my fear' as though it were, rather than 'loathsome', a thing of value, 'a diamond ring'. This symbol of engagement between human and roach startles the poet into seeing the creature anew as the young woman 'held [it] up to the light'.[15]

Rukeyser's 'St Roach' (*The Gates*, 1976) shows the metamorphosis occurring in the poet's mind as she realizes she has judged the cockroach without actually knowing it. Her response is altered when, 'for the first time', she really looks at an individual roach. Suddenly it acquires personality, seeming 'troubled and witty'. The next day, for the first time, she touches one of the roaches. Instead of being repulsed, she finds herself reaching out to 'begin to know you'. Then the poem becomes a prayer for forgiveness for exactly the human flaws Perkins exposes in *Bob Bridges*: losing touch with the natural world and its beings.[16]

Rukeyser's and Sexton's insight is echoed in the diamond facets of the moon in Jane Smiley's 'Gregor: My Life as a Bug', as well as in the golden wedding band that becomes a central symbol in Anna Castillo's 'Christmas Story of the Golden Cockroach' and in the startling photographs of Catherine Chalmers.

In Jane Smiley's novel *Moo* (1995), a professor of creative writing claims:

> Gregor Samsa is redeemed by being turned into a bug in that he learned to live in the physical world, and take pleasure in simple actions like running over the walls of his room or hanging from the ceiling and rocking back and forth. Being turned into a bug is a step UP for him.[17]

Three years earlier, her short story 'My Life as a Bug' illustrates the point. Smiley's Gregor, like Marc Estrin's Gregor, not dead at all, awakens in the dust-heap where the family's house-keeper has disposed of him. Rather than seeming outsized and monstrous (views that reflected his family's and society's views of cockroaches), he and the landscape around him have been transformed by the light of the moon. He sees through the new, many-faceted eyes of the cockroach and the moonlight and notes, echoing Sexton's poem, that the moon now appears 'not flat but full of facets like a great diamond'. And suddenly he sees his life, instead of ended, as full of possibilities, something he had never felt as a human.[18]

Because of that association with life, in her poem 'Natural Selection', Vivian Shipley turns naturally to the cockroach as a positive association after describing the mindless killing of 'A beetle, large/shiny as a cockroach', and poet Gwynn Popovac, encountering a cockroach in her bathroom sink late at night, is not alarmed but fascinated as, rather than fleeing, it continues to 'draw its long, elegant antennae through its/meticulous little mouth'. It strikes her that it,

. . . like the licking cat,
the preening bird, and
the human with a
soapy washcloth . . .
. . . wishes to be clean.[19]

A similar note is sounded in 'The Survivor' (2002) by poet Maxine Kumin. Having observed the cockroach's journey with man 'on/the long climb from savagery/to civilization' and their long history together, Kumin condemns human treatment of the cockroach. Calling the cockroach our 'spurned lover', she envisions that, in spite of us,

After the final call to arms
after we all go under
she alone will lurk, hatching babies
to feed on the charred remains
of our apocalyptic blunder.[20]

Both Tina Carvalho and Catherine Chalmers produce photographic images of the cockroach that question human attitudes toward the insect and ask for revaluation. Carvalho's enhanced electron microscopic images and Chalmers's first series of cockroach photographs, *Imposters*, emphasized how colourful and appealing many species of cockroach are. Perhaps as important as what the work of these women depicts are the methods they use to obtain their photographs. Whereas other cockroach artists like Richard Boscarino and Barbara Norfleet use dead specimens, Chalmers's are frozen, posed and photographed only when they have begun to revive. Both Chalmers and Carvalho are interested in the living creature rather than an easily manipulated model and use their photographic skills much as did the early twentieth-century film innovator Percy Smith to celebrate the underdog and reveal the beauty of the beastly.

Women artists are not alone in embracing the cockroach as an ecofeminist icon. Kafka himself probably anticipates that perspective. And cockroaches become symbols for a biocentric ethic akin to that of many indigenous peoples in the work of male fiction writers as diverse as William Gass and Donald Harington. Gass's 'Order of Insects' traces a housewife's metamorphosis from cockroach-hater to respectful appreciator. Like Sue Hubbell in *A Country Year*, Gass's housewife begins 'to stoop down beside them and take a closer look',[21] not only at the cockroach but at the whole insect world. It reveals itself as not inferior to hers but more full of beauty and meaning, its inhabitants revealed as the possessors of lives richer by far than her own:

> I could go away like the wise cicada who abandons its shell to move to other mischief. I could leave and let my bones play cards and spank the children . . . Peace. How can I think of such ludicrous things – beauty and peace, the dark soul of the world – for I am the wife of the house, concerned for the rug, tidy and punctual, surrounded by blocks.[22]

In *The Cockroaches of Stay More* (1989), Donald Harington 'crawls inside the minds of cockroaches and gives [his readers] an unexpected look at [both them and] ourselves', wrote a *Washington Post* reviewer. His Stay More is an all but deserted village in the Ozarks of Arkansas. Its cockroaches are steeped in the culture of the first humans to settle among these hills, represented in the novel by what Harington calls the Purple Symphony, music made up of the sounds and smells of the natural world.

Harington's 'roosterroaches', like Perkin's and Estrin's protagonists, fear the advent of 'the Bomb'. Like Perkins, Harington suggests that the descendants of the present cockroaches 'would lead Stay More through the post-Bomb period and pave the way for a new Golden Age'.[23] Similarly, Estrin's twenty-first-century Gregor sees war as man's 'profound failure . . . to find a right way to live'.[24] As an adviser to the researchers in Los Alamos, Estrin's cockroach protagonist finds himself resonating to the animal-gods of the Taos peoples. It seems to him if he could 'suspend . . . human thought . . . a surge of divinity might come streaming through him' and he wishes to express it as the Indians do with a Roach Dance.

Gregor Samsa Ingledew is the cockroach protagonist of Donald Harington's novel of 1989.

An Indian friend, intent on showing him the wisdom of his new insight, takes him to see the petroglyphs his ancestors created:

> At about five-thirty, the figure on the stone began . . . to grow . . . antennae! Gregor was doubtful at first, but as the sun sank lower, there was no doubt: two lightly feathered antennae slowly appeared from the previously unadorned head. Next . . . a third pair of limbs, growing

high out of the thorax, reaching in praise to the sky! The final touch – at six-thirty – little hooks appeared at the end of all the limbs, and a set of cercae emerged at the bottom of the abdomen. Six forty-five – the metamorphosis was complete: a man had turned into an insect![25]

When Gregor subsequently immolates himself at ground-zero of a pre-Hiroshima bomb test, he does so because he acknowledges himself as 'THE ROACH OF THE GOD CARBONIFEROUS, A LIVING RUMOR OF ETERNITY.' His action earns him an immortality not unlike that earned by Aristophanes' cockroach in *Peace*, some 2,500 years earlier. Like Perkins's post-apocalypse cockroaches, Estrin's Gregor offers himself as a sacrifice to teach man to seek redemption before it is too late. Like them he offers himself to lead us to rediscover our animal (or insect) selves and our place in the natural world. Something of the same hope echoes, despite the poem's initial horrible cockroach sighting, in C. K. Williams's 'Fear'.

While that initial sighting recalls first the nuclear terror of his youth and associates it with the current 'politics of terror', the poet concludes that 'Vermin, poison, atrocious deaths' have come to have a 'different resonance' for twenty-first-century man, we who have come to acknowledge ourselves rather than the other as the guilty one – or at least a sharer of guilt. That acknowledgement turns the roach-like grackles and, by association, the roaches themselves into something 'eerily otherworldly'. Their 'rich sheen' seems, like the 'iridescence' of the golden cockroach, to have 'risen from some counter-realm to rescue us'.[26]

In Estrin's novel, after Gregor's death, the Hospital Director at the Manhattan Project summarizes the theme both of *Insect Dreams* and Williams's 'Fear': 'the really "new frontier" of our age will not be defined politically. It will be delineated only by a revolution in our instinctual lives comparable to the Industrial Revolution. This is why Gregor's life, his example, held such great promise . . . We may still be saved by obscure efforts of heroic individuals whose passion it is to redeem the world.'[27] Williams's poem 'Fear' ends with the warning that we must seize the magic moment because, even as we recognize it as our salvation, the grackles and roaches are scattering 'toward some deepening darkness', threatening to leave us alone to our fate.

As so many ecofeminist writers have assured us, we are not alone. Ecofeminism urges us, as does the narrator of Linda Hogan's 'Small Life', to surrender to the night music of insects. The cockroach's story teaches us our place in nature's symphony exactly because 'the true soul of the roach . . . [i]s the same as the dark soul of the world itself'.[28] Listening to that ancient soul and voice, we can gain its secret wisdom, embracing the fertile soil of the chthonic earth as our animistic ancestors did without the fear it now holds for us. Indeed, our survival as a species may depend on discovering a saviour who looks at us from many-faceted eyes that replace our own myopic human view with the cockroach's 'very long view indeed'.[29]

The cockroach overview on human nature and human affairs continues.

Timeline of the Cockroach

450–400 MILLION BC

Probable emergence of
the first cockroach

400–300 MILLION BC

Carboniferous period:
the age of the cock-
roach. Fossils of at
least 800 distinct
species from the era
have been collected
and identified to date

65 MILLION BC

K.T. Dinosaur extinction: the cockroach survives as it had survived
six prior global extinctions and the
eight since, gaining the cockroach
its reputation as a survivor

AD 30–80

Pliny and others
record medicinal uses
of the cockroach,
beginning a long
history of scientific
observation and
comment

1492

Columbus sails with 'cucarachas'
aboard, introducing Old World
'pests' to the New World indigenous species (or, reuniting species
separated when Pangaea drifted
apart)

1587

Sir Francis Drake introduces those
same 'pest' species to England when
he brings the pirated *San Felipe* to
harbour in London; Thomas Mouffet
includes the
'cacarootch' in his
two volume *Theatre
of Insects* (1665),
the first modern
scientific account
of the cockroach

1944–1966

The Nonfictional Cockroach hits the
American popular press: Edwin Way
Teal's 'superbug' appears in *Collier's*
magazine; Howard Evan's 'The
Intellectual and Emotional World of
the Cockroach' appears in *Harper's*

1982–1991

Founding of British Blattadae Culture Group; Daniel Evan
Weiss's novel *Unnatural Selection* is published in London
(in the USA as *The Roaches Have No King*, 1994); James
Hillman's 'Going Bugs' appears in Jungian psychology
journal; Donald Harington's novel *The Cockroaches of Stay
More* published; opening of the films *Twilight of the
Cockroaches* from Japan and *The Nest*; Jay Mechling's 'From
archy to Archy: Why Cockroaches are Good to Think'
appears; *Joe's Apartment* short subject debuts on MTV

2–3 MILLION BC	1750–1300 BC	620–560 BC	422 BC
Emergence of humans, the cockroach's favorite fellow-traveller. By this time cockroaches are established in virtually every ecological niche the planet affords	Egyptian *Book of the Dead* offers prayer against cockroach infestation and the recorded war between man and cockroach commences	Aesop writes a fable telling of the cock-roach's revenge against the eagle for killing his friend, the hare, and the cock-roach enters human lore as a positive, even heroic, character	A heroic cockroach plays a major role in Aristophanes' anti-war play *Peace* and is rewarded with immortality, joining Pegasus in the Olympian stables

1869	1912–15	1929	1937
T. H. Huxley proclaims the cockroach the archetypal insect, the model from which all other insects evolved!	C. H. Turner's experiment prove the intelligence of the cockroach; the first of Marquis's 'archy' columns appears in the *New York Sun*; Kafka's *Die Verwandlung* published in Germany: a new Age of the Cockroach begins	Marquis's *archy and mehitabel* appears as a book, the first of many volumes in English in which a cockroach is both narrator and character	Kafka's *Metamorphosis* is translated and published in English 

1996–9	2000–2002	2003
David George Gordon's *The Complete Cockroach* published; *Mimic* and *Men in Black* premier in movie theaters; first edition of Joanne Luack's *The Voice of the Infinite in the Small* published; Penny Perkins's apocalyptic novel *Bob Bridges* published; Richard Schweid's *The Cockroach Papers* published	Janelle Cannon's *Crickwing* brings cockroaches to children and B.I.O. Bugs infest the toy market; Marc Estrin's *Insect Dreams: The Half-Life of Gregor Samsa* published; Lalo Alcaraz's daily cartoon strip, *La Cucaracha* syndicated	Catherine Chalmers's exhibit, 'American Cockroach', opens at the Rare Gallery, New York City: drawings, photographs, sculptures and videos championing the 21st-century cockroach

Appendix: *La Cucaracha*

Cuando uno quiere a una
Y esta una no lo quiere,
Es lo mismo que si un calvo
En la calle encuentr' un peine.

Chorus:
La cucaracha, la cucaracha,
Ya no quieres caminar,
Porque no tienes,
Porque le falta,
Marihuana que fumar.

Las muchachas so de oro;
Las casadas son de plata;
Las viudas son de cobre,
Y las viejas oja de lata.

Mi vecina de enfrente
Se llamaba Doña Clara,
Y si no había muerto
Es probable se llamara.

Las muchachas de la villa
No saben ni dar un beso,
Cuando las de Albuquerque
Hasta estiran el pescuezo.

Las muchachas Mexicanas
Son lindas como una flor,
Y hablan tan dulcemente
Que encantan de amor.

Una cosa me da risa –
Pancho Villa sin camisa.
Ya se van los Carranzistas
Porque vienen los Villistas.

Necesita automóvil
Par' hacer la caminata
Al lugar a donde mandó
La convención Zapata.

When a fellow loves a maiden
And that maiden doesn't love him,
It's the same as when a bald man
Finds a comb upon the highway.

Chorus:
The cucaracha, the cucaracha,
Doesn't want to travel on
Because she hasn't,
Oh no, she hasn't,
Marihuana for to smoke.

All the maidens are of pure gold;
All the married girls are silver;
All the widows are of copper,
And old women merely tin.

My neighbour across the highway
Used to be called Doña Clara,
And if she has not expired
Likely that's her name tomorrow.

All the girls here in the city
Don't know how to give you kisses,
While the ones from Albuquerque
Stretch their necks to avoid misses.

All the girls from Mexico
Are as pretty as a flower
And they talk so very sweetly,
Fill your heart quite up with love.

One thing makes me laugh most hearty –
Pancho Villa with no shirt on
Now the Carranzistas beat it
Because Villa's men are coming.

Fellow needs an automobile
If he undertakes the journey
To the place to which Zapata
Ordered the famous convention.

References

INTRODUCTION

1 Stephen Jay Gould, 'Introduction: A Flawed Work in Progress', in *The Book of Life*, 2nd revd edn (New York and London, 2001), p. 10.
2 Don Marquis, *archy and mehitabel*, illus. George Harriman (New York, 1990 edn), p. 58.
3 Steven Bodio, 'Introduction', to John Crompton, *The Hunting Wasp* (New York, 1993 edn), pp. vi, vii.
4 Joanne Elizabeth Luack, *The Voice of the Infinite in the Small: Revisioning the Insect–Human Connection* (Mill Spring, NY, 1998), p. 89.
5 David Abram, *The Spell of the Sensuous: Perception and Language in a More–than–Human World* (New York, 1996), p. 4; May Berenbaum, *Bugs in the System: Insects and their Impact on Human Affairs* (Reading, MA, 1995), p. xii; Luack, *The Voice of the Infinite in the Small*, p. 86.
6 Abram, *The Spell of the Sensuous*, p. 121.
7 Steven Kellert, 'Values and Perceptions of Invertebrates', *Conservation Biology*, 7 (December 1993), p. 853.

1 A LIVING FOSSIL

1 Michael Benton, 'Dinosaur Summer', in Stephen Jay Gould ed., *The Book of Life*, 2nd revd edn (New York and London, 2001), p. 157.

2 See Carl Zimmer's *Parasite Rex: Inside the Bizarre World of Nature's Most Dangerous Creatures* (New York, 2000).

3 These driver/army ant–cockroach encounter narratives come from: Charles Darwin, *The Voyage of the Beagle* (New York, 1988 [1836]), p. 29; Henry Walter Bates, *The Naturalist on the River Amazon* [1863] (New York, 1988), p. 345; Marty Crump, *In Search of the Golden Frog* (Chicago and London, 2000), pp. 146–7; Robert Sapolsky, *A Primate's Memoir: A Neuroscientist's Unconventional Life Among the Baboons* (New York, 2001), pp. 156–7.

4 Natalie Angier, *The Beauty of the Beastly: New Views on the Nature of Life* (New York and Boston, 1996), p. 118.

5 Lisa Drew, 'Creatures that Time Forgot', *National Wildlife*, 40 (June–July 2002), p. 30.

6 Bernd Heinrich, *The Thermal Warriors: Strategies of Insect Survival* (Cambridge, MA and London, 1996), p. 21.

7 Quoted in Sy Montgomery, *Journey of the Pink Dolphins: An Amazon Quest* (New York, 2000), pp. 162–3, 181–2, 186–7.

8 Richard Fortey, *Life: A Natural History of the First Four Billion Years of Life on Earth* (New York, 1998), p. 167.

9 Heinrich, *The Thermal Warriors*, p. 13.

10 Daniel Evan Weiss, *The Roaches Have No King* (New York and London, 1994), p. 60. I sometimes rely on novelists as well as scientists for the natural history and biology of the cockroach, I have found that, in order to create as authentic cockroach characters as writers like Weiss do, they have done the requisite research and, in their novels present it in a straightforward, effective way.

11 Louis Barbier, 'The Cucaracha Wars', www.czbrats.com/story/cucaracha.htm.

12 Weiss, *The Roaches Have No King*, pp. 186–7.

13 John Kricher, *A Neotropical Companion: An Introduction to the Animals, Plants & Ecology of the New World Tropics*, 2nd edn (Princeton, NJ, 1997), p. 350.

14 Weiss, *The Roaches Have No King*, p. 165.

15 L. C. Miall and Albert Denny, *The Structure and Life Story of the Cockroach (Periplaneta orientalis)* (London, 1886) quoted in David Quammen, 'A Republic of Cockroaches: When the Ultimate Exterminator Meets the Ultimate Pest', in *Natural Acts: A Sidelong View of Science and Nature* (New York, 1985), p. 54.

16 Steven Cousins, *Frankenbug!* (New York, 2000), p. 109.

17 Marc Estrin, *Insect Dreams: The Half–Life of Gregor Samsa* (New York, 2002), pp. 11–12.

18 Estrin, *Insect Dreams*, p. 11.

19 Allen Moore,' R+D: News about Science, Medicine and Technology', *Discover*, 19 (February 1998), p. 9.

20 Gerald Durrell with Lee Durrell, *A Practical Guide for the Amateur Naturalist* (New York, 1988), p. 26.

21 Donald Harington, *The Cockroaches of Stay More* (New York, 1989), p. 45.

22 Estrin, *Insect Dreams*, p. 11.

23 Cousins, *Frankenbug!*, p. 108.

24 BBC News online, 17 February 1999.

25 H. Elizabeth Braker and Harry W. Greene, 'Population Biology: Life Histories, Abundance, Demography, and Predator–Prey Interactions', in Lucinda A. McDade et al., *La Selva: Ecology and Natural History of a Neotropical Rainforest* (Chicago and London, 1994), p. 249.

26 David Rains Wallace, *Idle Weeds: The Life of a Sandstone Ridge* (San Francisco, 1980), p. 175.

27 Edward O. Wilson, 'The Evolutionary Significance of Social Insects', in David Pemental, ed., *Insects, Science, and Society* (New York, San Francisco and London, 1975), pp. 29–39.

28 Tom Wakefield, *The Liaisons of Life: From Hornworms to Hippos, How the Unassuming Microbe Has Driven Evolution* (New York, 2001), pp. 145, 153.

29 Gilbert Waldbauer, *Millions of Monarchs, Bunches of Beetles: How Bugs Find Strength in Numbers* (Cambridge, MA and London, 2000), p. 4.

30 David George Gordon, *The Compleat Cockroach: A Comprehensive Guide to the Most Despised (and least Understood) Creature on Earth* (New York, 1996), p. 27.

31 Quoted in Jonathan Maslow, *Footsteps in the Jungle: Adventures in the Scientific Exploration of the Tropics* (Chicago, 1996), p. 128.

32 Edwin Way Teale, 'Superbug', *Collier's* (11 March 1944), pp. 20–21.

2 WHAT'S IN A NAME?

1 Gustav Eckstein, 'I Began to Call Her Minnie', *Everyday Miracle* [1934] (New York, 1948), p. 227.

2 Gordon's Blattodea Page: www.earthlife.net/insects/blatodal.html.

3 Peter Landesmon, 'A Woman's Work', *The New York Times Magazine* (15 September 2002), p. 31.

4 'What's So Bad About Hate?': www.andrewsullivan.com.

5 Richard Schweid, *The Cockroach Papers: A Compendium of History and Lore* (New York and London, 1999), p. 29.

6 http://yucky.kids.discovery/.com/flash/roaches/.

7 Daniel Evan Weiss, *The Roaches Have No King* (New York and London, 1994), p. 6.

8 Martin Locke, Harry Leung and Michael Locke, 'Ancient and Modern Illustrations in Entomology', in Jill Adams, ed., *Insect Potpourri: Adventures in Entomology* (Gainsville, FL, 1992), p. 258.

9 Keith Thomas, *Man and the Natural World: A History of Modern Sensibility* (New York, 1983), pp. 84, 57–8, 91.

10 Sue Hubbell, *Waiting for Aphrodite: Journeys Into the Time Before Bones* (New York and Boston, 1999), p. 154.

11 Howard Ensign Evans, 'The Intellectual and Emotional World of the Cockroach', *Life on a Little-Known Planet: A Biologist's View of Insects and their World* (New York, 1993), p. 61.

12 Ann Hornaday, 'Roach Fever', *Ms* (October 1986), p. 98.

13 Joy Massoff, *Oh, Yuck! The Encyclopaedia of Everything Nasty* (New York, 2000), pp. 31–2.

14 Bernd Heinrich, *The Thermal Warriors: Strategies of Insect Survival* (Cambridge, MA and London, 1996), p. 196.

15 Gordon, *The Complete Cockroach*, pp.xiii–xiv.

3 FELLOW TRAVELLER

1 Gordon, *The Compleat Cockroach*, pp. 37, 39.

2 www.qmuseum.geld.gov.au/.

3 Amy Reiter, 'Run, Roaches, Run', www.salon.com/people/col/reit/1999/08/19/reitthar.html

4 Mark Twain, *Roughing It* [1890] (New York and London, 1980), pp. 373–4.

5 Dan Simmons, *Fires of Eden* (New York, 1994), pp. 66–7.

6 Isabella Bird, *The Golden Chersonese* (Cologne, 2000), pp. 126, 213.

7 Jack London, *The Cruise of the Snark: A Pacific Voyage* [1911] (London and New York, 1986), pp. 263, 301.

8 Ronald Wright, *Henderson's Spear* (New York, 2002), pp. 3, 328.

9 Quoted in Richard Schweid, *The Cockroach Papers: A Compendium of History and Lore* (New York and London, 1999), p. 86.

10 Henry Walter Bates, *The Naturalist on the River Amazon* (New York, 1988 [1863]), pp. 65, 195.

11 Quoted in Douglas Daily, 'The Perils of Collecting', *Audubon*, 97 (January–February 1995), pp. 79–80.

12 Sy Montgomery, *Journey of the Pink Dolphin: An Amazon Quest* (New York and London, 2000), pp. 113, 146.

13 Marty Crump, *The Search for the Golden Frog* (Chicago and

London, 2000), p. 79.

14 John Crompton, *The Hunting Wasp* [1955] (New York, 1987),
    pp. 67–9.

15 allthingskenyan.crosswinds.net/cockroachcaper.html.

16 Peter Tyson, *The Eighth Continent: Life, Death, and Discovery in
    the Lost World of Madagascar* (New York, 2000), pp. 1, 39, 95.

17 Gerald Durrell with Lee Durrell, *A Practical Guide for the Amateur
    Naturalist* (New York, 1988), p. 26.

18 Elisavietta Ritchie, 'The Cockroach Hovered Like a Dirigible', *And
    a Deer's Ear, Eagle's Song and Bear's Grace: Animals and Women*, ed.
    Theresa Corrigan and Stephanie Hoppe (Pittsburgh, 1990),
    pp. 53-6.

19 Joanne Elizabeth Luack, *The Voice of the Infinite in the Small:
    Revisioning the Insect–Human Connection* (Mill Spring, NC, 1998),
    pp. 94–5.

20 Schweid, *The Cockroach Papers*, p. 2.

21 H-NILAS list, distributed 26 June 2001.

22 John Kricher, *A Neotropical Companion: An Introduction to the
    Animals, Plants & Ecology of the New World Tropics* (Princeton, NJ
    1997), p. 329.

23 John Hay, 'Sacred Places', in *The Immortal Wilderness* (New York
    and London, 1987), p. 162.

4 IN THE MIND OF MAN: MYTH, FOLKLORE AND THE ARTS

1 Richard Schweid, *The Cockroach Papers: A Compendium of History
    and Lore* (New York and London, 1999), p. 122.

2 Malcolm Davies and Jeyaraney Kathirithamby, *Greek Insects* (New
    York, 1986), pp. 3, 11–12, 86–7.

3 Joanne Elizabeth Luack, *The Voice of the Infinite in the Small:
    Revisioning the Insect–Human Connection* (Mill Spring, NC, 1998), p. 87.

4 James Hillman, 'Going Bugs', *Spring: A Journal of Archetype and*

Culture, (1988), p. 66.

5   Philip M. Tierno, *The Secret Life of Germs: Observations and Lessons from a Microbe Hunter* (New York, 2001), pp. 165, 167, 169.

6   J. L. Cloudsley-Thompson, *Insects and History* (New York, 1976), p. 204.

7   Schweid, *The Cockroach Papers*, p. 119.

8   Julie Hughes, 'Quit Bugging Me! Suggestions for a Roach Free Life', *Spring: A Journal of Archetype and Culture* (January 1997).

9   Douglas A. Preston and Lincoln Child, *The Cabinet of Curiosities* (New York, 2002), p. 420.

10 Allan Baillie, 'The Taste of Cockroach', in *The Taste of Cockroach and Other Stories*, ed. John Griffin and Warwick Goodenough.

11 www.stars.com/lifestyle/101706098373366.html.

12 Alexis Rockmann, 'Standard Exterminating [Interview with Gil Bloom]', in Mark Dion and Alexis Rockmann, eds, *Concrete Jungle: A Pop Media Investigation of Death and Survival in Urban Ecosystems* (New York, 1996), p. 28.

13 James Eckle, 'Road Kills, Road Eats', in Dion and Rockmann, eds, *Concrete Jungle*, p. 187.

14 Christopher S. Wren, *The Cat Who Covered the World: The Adventures of Henrietta and Her Foreign Correspondent*, illus. Meilo So (New York, 2001), pp. 138–9, 163.

15 Roger D. Abrahams, ed., *Afro–American Folktales: Stories from Black Traditions in the New World* (New York, 1985), pp. 163–4.

16 Don Marquis, *archy and mehitabel*, illus. George Harriman (New York, 1990 [1927]), p. 128.

17 Betty O'Grady, 'Tchicaya U Tam'si: Some Thoughts on the Poet's Symbolic Mode of Expression', *World Literature Today*, 65 (Winter 1991), pp. 29–34.

18 www.wits.ac.za/emergence/new_103.htm.

19 Thom Harrison, NILAS list, 27 March 2002 (h-nilas@h-net.msu.edu).

20 Dieter P. Lotze, 'Of Cockroaches and Civilizing Hungary: Imre Madach as an Aristotelian Satirist', *Neohelicon*, 106 (1988), p. 209.

21 Howard Ensign Evans, 'The Intellectual and Emotional World of the Cockroach', *Life on a Little-Known Planet: A Biologist's View of Insects and their World* (New York, 1993), p. 49.

22 Sarah Scalet, 'The Cosmopolitan Cockroach', *Audubon*, 101 (September–October 1999), p. 52.

23 Sue Hubbell, *A Country Year: Living the Questions* [1983] (Boston and New York, 1999), p. 137.

24 www.pestshop.com.

25 Gordon, *The Compleat Cockroach*, p. 132.

26 David Browne, 'Family Values', *Entertainment Weekly*, (21 June 2002), pp. 81–2.

27 Trevor Todd, *The Cockroach Who Wrote a Symphony*, illus. Thomas Trahair (Sydney, 1979), p. 17.

5 TALES FROM THE UNDERSIDE

1 Fergus M. Bordewich, 'Manhattan Mayhem', *Smithsonian*, 34 (December 2002), pp. 50, 44–54; Adam Gopnik, 'A Critic at Large: "Underworld: Herbert Ashby's Irresistible Histories"', *The New Yorker* (8 November 2002), p. 176.

2 Sarah Boxer, as quoted in Boria Sax, *The Mythical Zoo: An Encyclopedia of Animals in World Myth, Legend, and Literature* (Santa Barbara, CA, Denver, CO, and Oxford, England, 2002), p. xviii.

3 Richard Schweid, *The Cockroach Papers: A Compendium of History and Lore* (New York and London, 1999), p. 27.

4 Shirley Rousseau Murphy, *Cat Spitting Mad* (New York, 2001), p. 123. Representing the nonhuman underdog or cat would please the cockroach, I think, just as efforts on the parts of cockroach supporters like comic strip great Birke Breathed to promote

'Cockroach Rights' and to confront readers with appealing non-human characters like his cockroach Milquetoast would please the totem of the under-appreciated.

5 Pedro Pietri, 'Suicide Note from a Cockroach in a Low Income Housing Development', *Puerto Rican Obituary*, (New York, 1970).

6 Martin Espada, 'Cockroaches of Liberation', *City of Coughing and Dead Radiators* (New York, 1993).

7 Eugene J. McCarthy, 'Roaches Take Over New York City Buses', *Ground Fog and Night* (New York and London, 1979), p. 43.

8 Margo Jefferson, 'It's Hot! Bring Me a Book!', *The New York Times Book Review* (7 July 2002), p. 23.

9 Daniel Evan Weiss, *The Roaches Have No King* (New York and London, 1994).

10 Brian M. Wiprud, 'Ratville,' in Mark Dion and Alexis Rockmann, eds, *Concrete Jungle: A Pop Media Investigation of Death and Survival in Urban Ecosystems* (New York, 1996), p. 157.

11 'Fear', *The New York Times* (29 August 2002), A25.

12 Quoted in Schweid, *The Cockroach Papers*, pp. 100–101.

13 Gillian Tindall, *Countries of the Mind: The Meaning of Place to Writers* (London, 1991), p. 238.

14 Reza Ordoubadian, 'Kafka's Cockroach', published in *The Iranian* (April 2002), an online magazine (www.iranian.com).

15 Marc Estrin, *Insect Dreams: The Half–Life of Gregor Samsa* (New York, 2002), p. 171.

16 *Ibid.*, pp. 263–4.

17 Janus Glowacki 'Hunting Cockroaches', in *Hunting Cockroaches and Other Plays* (Evaston, IL, 1990), p. 77.

18 *The School Library Journal*, quoted on the back cover of Mary James, *Shoebag* (New York, 1990).

19 Christopher Morley, 'dedicated to don marquis', in Martha Paulos, ed. and illus., *Insect–Asides: Great Poems on Man's Pest*

Friends (New York, 1994), p. 2.

20 Dana Stabenow, *Play With Fire* (New York, 1995).

21 Jim Ennes's archie: www.halcyon.com/jim.

22 'The Week in Review', *The New York Times* (21 April 2002), p. 6.

6 ROBO-ROACH

1 Stephen M. Wise, *Drawing the Line: Science and the Case for Animals Rights* (Cambridge, MA, 2002), p. 73.

2 Lori Oliwenstein, 'The Bug that Can Say No', *Discover* (23 April 2002), p. 76.

3 Charles Siebert, 'What the Roaches Told Her', *The New York Times Magazine* (31 December 1995), p. 27.

4 Daniel Evan Weiss, *The Roaches Have No King* (New York and London, 1994), p. 118.

5 *Ibid.*, p. 121.

6 www:users.ren.com/Heirman/roach/html.

7 Lynn Margulis and Dorion Sagan, *Mystery Dance: On the Evolution of Human Sexuality* (New York, 1992), p. 185.

8 Jay Mechling, 'From archy to Archy: Why Cockroaches are Good to Think', *Southern Folklore*, 48 (1991), p. 131.

9 May R. Berenbaum, *Bugs in the System: Insects and their Impact on Human Affairs* (Reading, MA, 1995), pp. 332.

10 members.aol.com/Kaltofen/aolMKroach.html.

11 Richard Meyers, *The World of Fantasy Films* (New York, 1980), p. 102.

12 Thomas Disch, *The Dreams Our Stuff is Made Of: How Science Fiction Conquered the World* (New York, 1998), pp. 96–7.

13 Joanne Elizabeth Luack, *The Voice of the Infinite in the Small: Revisioning the Insect–Human Connection* (Mill Spring, NC, 1998), p. 5.

14 Ray Sawhill, 'Overlooked Roach Motel', *Newsweek* (25 August 1997), p. 72. Wells's novel may indeed be the earliest appearance of mutant cockroaches in science fiction.

15 John G. Nettles, review of Lance Olsen's *Sewing Shut My Eyes* (PopMatters:www.Popmatters.com/books/reviews/s/sewing-shut-my-eyes.html).

16 Dave Barry, 'Six Legs and a Bad Attitude Not Good Enough for Some', *Miami Herald* (9 July 1995).

17 Fenella Saunders, 'Brainy Bots', *Discover* (23 April 2002), p. 76.

18 Boadicea: www.ai.mit.edu/projects/boadicea/boadicea.html.

7 THE GOLDEN COCKROACH

1 James Gorman, 'A Wild World Beneath Each Leaf', *The International Herald Tribune Online* (26 September 2003).

2 All Species Project Online: www.all–species.org.

3 Caroline Alexander, *One Dry Season: In the Footsteps of Mary Kingsley* (New York, 1991), p. 202.

4 Kilgore Trout [Kurt Vonnegut], *Venus on the Half–Shell* (Cutchogue, NY, 1974), p. 203.

5 Christopher Blayre, 'The Blue Cockroach', in *The Purple Sapphire and Other Posthumous Papers: Selected from the Unofficial Records of the University of Cosmopoli by Christopher Blayre, Sometime Register of the University* (London, 1921), p. 130.

6 Virginia Museum of Natural History: www.vmnh.org/bug1196.html.

7 Luack, *The Voice of the Infinite in the Small*, p. 309.

8 Rachel Carson, *The Sense of Wonder* [1956] (New York, 1984).

9 Gordon, *The Compleat Cockroach*, p. 119.

10 Daniel Massa, 'Interview with Francis Eberje', *World Literature Written in English*, 2 (1984), p. 480.

11 Penny Perkins, *Bob Bridges: An Apocalyptic Fable* (Albany, NY, 1999), p. 155.

12 Caroline Frazer, 'Ratty Go Batty', *The New Yorker* (5 December 1994), p. 102.

13 Perkins, *Bob Bridges*, p. 49.

14 Linda Hogan, 'Small Life', in Theresa Corrigan and Stephanie Hoppe, eds, *And a Deer's Ear, Eagle's Song and Bear's Grace: Animals and Women* (Pittsburg, 1990), p. 52.

15 Anne Sexton, 'Cockroach', *45 Mercy Street* (Boston, 1974), p. 38.

16 Muriel Rukeyser, 'St Roach', *The Collected Poems of Muriel Rukeyser* (New York, 1978), p. 530.

17 Jane Smiley, *Moo* [1995] (New York, 1998), p. 237.

18 Jane Smiley, 'Gregor: My Life as a Bug', *Harper's Magazine* (August 1992).

19 Vivian Shipley, 'Natural Selection', *Poems Out of Harlan County* (Ithaca, NY, 1989), p. 21; Gwen Popovac, *Conversations With Bugs: A Journal with Words and Drawings* (San Francisco, 1993).

20 Maxine Kumin, 'The Survivor', *Hunger Mountain*, 1 (Fall 2002), p. 49.

21 Sue Hubbell, *A Country Year: Living the Questions* [1983] (Boston and New York, 1999), p. 137.

22 William Gass, 'Order of Insects', *In the Heart of the Heart of the Country and Other Stories* [1981] (Boston, 2000), p. 171.

23 Donald Harington, *The Cockroaches of Stay More* (New York, 1989), p. 198.

24 Marc Estrin, *Insect Dreams: The Half-Life of Gregor Samsa* (New York, 2002), p. 26.

25 *Ibid.*, pp. 334–5, 340, 426.

26 C. K. Williams, 'Fear', *The New York Times* (29 August 2002), p. A25.

27 Estrin, *Insect Dreams*, p. 461.

28 Gass, 'Order of Insects, p. 171.

29 As Sue Hubbel has observed in *A Country Year*, 'having in my cabin a harmless visitor whose structure evolution has barely touched since the Upper Carboniferous days strikes me . . . as a highly instructive event. Two hundred and fifty million years, after all, is a very long time indeed.'

Bibliography

Abram, David. *The Spell of the Sensuous: Perceptions and Language in a More-than-Human World* (New York, 1996)

Adams, Jill, ed., *Insect Potpourri: Adventures in Entomology* (Gainsville, FL, 1992)

Angier, Natalie. 'There is Nothing Like a Roach' in *The Beauty of the Beastly: New Views of the Nature of Life* (New York and Boston, 1996) pp. 116–21

Berenbaum, May R. *Bugs in the System: Insects and Their Impact on Human Affairs* (Reading, MA, 1995)

Cannon, Janelle, *Crickwing* (San Diego, New York and London, 2000)

Cloudsley-Thomson, J. L., *Insects and History* (New York, 1976)

Estrin, Marc, *Insect Dreams: The Half Life of Gregor Samsa* (New York, 2002)

Evans, Howard Ensign, 'The Intellectual and Emotional World of the Cockroach', *Harper's* (December 1966), pp. 50–55

—, *Life on a Little-Known Planet: A Biologist's View of Insects and the World* [1963] (New York, 1993) pp. 48–61.

Fitzhugh, Bill, *Pest Control* (New York, 1997)

Fortey, Richard, *Life: A Natural History of the First Four Billion Years of Life on Earth* (New York, 1998)

Gordon, David George, *The Compleat Cockroach: A Comprehensive Guide to the Most Despised (and Least*

Understood) Creature on Earth (New York, 1996)

Gould, Stephen J., ed., *The Book of Life*, 2nd revd edn (New York and London, 2001)

Harington, Donald, *The Cockroaches of Stay More* (New York, 1989)

Helfer, Jacques R., *How to Know the Grasshoppers, Crickets, Cockroaches and Their Allies* (New York, 1963)

Hillman, James. 'Going Bugs'. *Spring: A Journal of Archetype and Culture* (Spring 1988), pp. 40–72

Kafka, Franz, 'The Metamorphosis' in *Franz Kafka: The Complete Stories* ed. Nahum N. Glatzer and trans. Joachin Neugroschel (New York, 1971)

Kellert, Steven, 'Values and Perceptions of Invertebrates', *Conservation Biology*, 7 (December 1993), pp. 845–55

Kricher, John, *A Neotropical Companion: An Introduction to the Animals, Plants, & Ecology of the New World Tropics*, 2nd edn, revised and expanded (Princeton, NJ, 1997)

Lauck, Joanne Elizabeth, *The Voice of the Infinite in the Small: Revisioning the Insect-Human Connection* (Mill Spring, NC, 1998)

Lecard, Martin. 'Old Acquaintance', *Sierra* (March–April 1996), p. 26.

McMonigle, O. and R. Willis, *Allpet Roaches: Care and Identification Handbook for the Pet and Feeder Cockroaches* (2000)

Marquis, Don, *archy and mehitabel*, illus. George Harriman (New York, 1990)

Mechling, Jay, 'From archy to Archy: Why Cockroaches Are Good to Think', *Southern Folklore*, 48 (1991), pp. 121–40

Page, Thomas, *The Hephaestus Plague* (New York, 1973)

Perkins, Penny, *Bob Bridges: An Apocalyptic Fable*, (Albany, NY, 1999)

Poinar, George and Roberta, *The Amber Forest: A Reconstruction of a Vanished World* (Princeton, NJ, 1999)

Pimentel, David, ed., *Insects, Science and Society* (New York, San Francisco and London, 1975)

Quammen, David, 'A Republic of Cockroaches: When the Ultimate Exterminator Meets the Ultimate Pest', in *Natural Acts: A Sidelong View of Science and Nature* (New York, 1985) pp. 53–8 (first published in *Outside*, May 1983)

Schweid, Richard, *The Cockroach Papers: A Compendium of History and Lore* (New York and London, 1999)

Teale, Edwin Way, 'Superbug', *Collier's* (11 March 1944), pp.20–21

Waldbauer, Gilbert, *Millions of Monarchs, Bunches of Beetles: How Bugs Find Strength in Numbers* (Cambridge, MA, and London, 2000)

Weiss, Daniel Evan, *The Roaches Have No King* (New York and London, 1994); first published in the UK as *Unnatural Selection* (London, 1990).

Wilson, Edward O., *Biophilia* (Cambridge, MA, and London, 1984)

Associations

BLATTODAE CULTURE GROUP
www.earthlife.net/insects/bcg.html

Founded in 1986 to 'promote the study and culture of
cockroaches worldwide'. Contact Adrian Durkin, 8 Foley
Road, Pedmore, Stourbridge, West Midlands, DY9 8RT,
England, UK

NILAS (NATURE IN LEGEND AND STORY) COCKROACH TOTEM
GROUP
www.h-net.org/~nilas/totem/roach.html

Founded by the author in the mid-1990s for the study of
the cockroach in world literature and culture. The NILAS
Bibliography site also contains an extensive bibliography
of cockroaches in the arts (approaches to literature).

Websites

Gordon's Blattodea page:
www.earthlife.nat/insects/blatodea.html

Joseph Kunkel's Cockroach Site (Biology, University of
Massachusetts, Amherst):
www.bio.mass.edu/biology/kunkel/cockroach.html

Official La Cucaracha Archive Website: uccomics.com

University of Nebraska Cockroach Picture Gallery:
www.pested.unl.edu/roachind.htm

The Yuckiest Site on the Internet:
http://yucky.kids.discovery/.com/flash/roaches/

Acknowledgements

The cockroaches and I owe debts of gratitude to more of our fellow creatures than I will remember to acknowledge here. However, I could not have written this book without the help and support of all the observers (scientists, travellers, nature writers, novelists, and poets, especially Maxine Kumin, whose 'The Survivor' appeared in response to the proposal for this book) and appreciators (Howard Ensign Evans, David George Gordon, Richard Schweid); the readers (the Animal series editor Jonathan Burt, Catherine Chalmers, Elizabeth Lawrence, Joanne Luack, Sy Montgomery and my partner Kathryn H. Holmes, all of whom encouraged and advised and, most important, seemed to enjoy what I have written); the artists (Joe Bullock, Tina Carvalho, Catherine Chalmers, Amy Bartlett Wright); the friends who became indefatigable watchers for cockroach news in sources I might otherwise have overlooked; and most of all my immediate family – canine, caprine, equine, human, feline, and 'wild' (even if Kathy did draw the line at extending the species boundary of our home to include a colony of Madagascar hissing roaches from the UMASS Entomology Department!) Thanks none the less to the Entomology Department at the University of Massachusetts, Amherst, for sharing their knowledge and insight and, most crucial, for providing the necessary hands-on relationship that brought the cockroaches I'd met in art fully to life for me and, I hope, for my readers. Finally, my thanks to those wise and wonderful beings, the cockroaches themselves, without whom it is safe to say this book would never have been dreamed of, far less written.

Photo Acknowledgements

The author and publishers wish to express their thanks to the below sources of illustrative material and/or permission to reproduce it. While every effort has been made to identify and credit copyright holders, we would like to apologize to anyone who has not been formally acknowledged.

Illustration from *The Amateur Naturalist*, by Gerald Durrell, copyright © 1982 by Gerald Durrell. Used by permission of Alfred A. Knopf, a division of Random House, Inc.: p. 29; illustration from Poinar, George Jr, and Poinar, Roberta, *The Amber Forest: A Reconstruction of a Vanished World*, copyright © 1999 Princeton University Press. Reprinted by permission of Princeton University Press: p. 17; illustration from *Archy and Mehitabel* by Don Marquis, copyright 1927 by Doubleday, a division of Random House, Inc., used by permission of Doubleday, a division of Random House, Inc.: pp. 122, 123; reproduced from *archyology: the long lost tales of archy and mehitabel* (Hanover and London: University Press of New England, 1996). Reprinted by permission of the University Press of New England: p. 124; reproduced courtesy of Sandi Bachom: p. 161; illustration from *The Book of Life: An Illustrated History of the Evolution of Life on Earth*, by Steven Jay Gould, General Editor. © 2001, 1993. Used by permission of W.W. Norton & Company, Inc.: p. 16; © Joseph

Cockroach, ill. by Dave Mitchell. St Petersburg, Florida (La Frey Press, 1984): p. 159; courtesy Walter Oltmann/Goodman Gallery: p. 93; illustration (from Mark Catesby's 1747 *Natural History of Carolina, Florida, and the Bahama Islands*) from Blum, Ann Shelby, *Picturing Nature*, © 1993 by Princeton University Press. Reprinted by permission of Princeton University Press: pp. 6, 51; illustrations courtesy of Brian Raszka: pp. 13, 82, 87; photo courtesy of the artist, Travis Sommerville and the Catharine Clark Gallery: p. 120; courtesy of Amy Bartlett Wright: pp. 35, 37, 46, 86, 94, 95.

REPRINT PERMISSIONS
Excerpt from 'Roaches Take Over New York City Buses' in *Ground Fog and Night*, copyright © 1979 by Eugene J. McCarthy, reprinted by permission of Harcourt, Inc. Excerpts from *The Roaches Have No King* by Daniel Evan Weiss, copyright © 1996 Daniel Evan Weiss, published by Serpent's Tail, London, 1996. Excerpts from *archy and mehitabel* by Don Marquis copyright © 1927 by Doubleday, a division of Random House, Inc. Used by permission of Doubleday, a division of Random House, Inc. Excerpts from *archyology: the long lost tales of archy and mehitabel* by Don Marquis; this compilation © 1998 by Jeff Adams; reprinted by permission of the University Press of New England. Excerpts from *Insect Dreams* © 2002 by Marc Estrin, reprinted by permission of Penguin Putnam Inc. Excerpts from *The Cockroaches of Stay More*, copyright © 1989 by Donald Harington, reprinted by permission of Harcourt, Inc. Excerpts from *The Cockroach Papers: A Compendium of History and Lore* by Richard Schweid, 1999, with permission by Four Walls Eight Windows. Excerpts from *A Country Year: Living the Questions* by Sue Hubbell, copyright © 1993 by Sue Hubbell, reprinted by permission of Houghton Mifflin Company. All rights reserved.

Index